learning
to eat along
the way

~ᴗᴖ~

A memoir

Margaret Bendet

SHE WRITES PRESS

Published 2015
Printed in the United States of America
ISBN: 978-1-63152-997-9
Library of Congress Control Number: 2015934891

For information, address:
She Writes Press
1563 Solano Ave #546
Berkeley, CA 94707

She Writes Press is a division of Spark Point Studio, LLC.

To my beloved teachers,
past and present,
and to the intrepid fellow travelers
I have been graced to meet along the way.

1. ᴄᴚ *Don't Talk to the Dead*

I FIRST HEARD THE VOICE in a room that was otherwise unremarkable—cream-colored walls, beige Berber carpet, bookshelves mounted on one wall, a worktable made from a salvaged door. It was our second bedroom, and my husband had designated it as my space. Initially, it was the place in the house where I could be messy, and I was messy there, until the night Tom took a couple of dinner guests through it to show them something in the storage closet beyond.

"Oh, this is Peggy's room," he explained as he led our friends, wide-eyed, through my chaos. Books and papers and materials for various crafts were stacked on the table and around the room on the floor, clothes (including underwear) from the last several days were piled on the two chairs, the closet door stood open. I felt outed, and outraged, but Tom had made his point. The next day I cleaned.

This room was where I worked on projects, and my latest project was learning to meditate. My hatha yoga teacher had added meditation at the end of our weekly classes, and I wanted to practice. I knew I wasn't doing it right. I couldn't be. It had to be more than just sitting and thinking.

I sat on the scratchy carpet in a half-lotus posture—cross-legged, with one foot under the other—closed my eyes, and took a deep breath in. I could hear the wind moving through the leaves of a tree just outside the window. I could hear the air going out through my nostrils. And behind that, in my mind,

I could hear a woman's voice, quavering but clear: *Get out of my house!*

I swallowed, opened my eyes, and stood up. I didn't leave the house, but I did leave the room. I went into the kitchen and started chopping onions and garlic for dinner, all the while pondering this disembodied voice.

I was nervous, disoriented, out of my depth. I worked in the features section of a daily newspaper, and I paid attention to what I heard. When someone spoke to me, I looked for cues—the expression on their face, their gestures, the tone of their voice, the place in their body from which they spoke. All of this told me what was going on behind the words: the questions behind a statement, the statements behind a question, the level of investment this person had in what they said, the authenticity with which they spoke. And all of this helped me know how to process what I'd heard, how to relate to it, how to respond.

But to hear just the voice . . .

Two things I knew immediately. First, I was sure it wasn't my imagination. I might have heard the words in my mind, but my mind had not created the words for me to hear. Why would it do such a thing? I hadn't thought about that woman for years—which brings me to the second thing I knew immediately. I knew who it was. Or, at least, to whom that voice had once belonged.

◆ ◆ ◆

SEVEN YEARS EARLIER, Tom and I had purchased this property from the adult children of a couple who had built the house for their retirement. Mr. and Mrs. Carter had lived in the house for some twenty-five years, and both had died there, Mr. Carter first and his wife following, about five years later.

The small frame house seemed perfect for Tom and me, and we both loved it on sight. It was painted a gray so light it looked like weathered wood. It was a ten-minute drive from downtown Honolulu, back in Manoa Valley, on the bottommost slopes of the storied Koolaus, with hibiscus bushes in the backyard and two huge sycamores in the front.

When we first moved in, Tom and I both had the feeling the original owners were still in residence. The place hadn't been thoroughly cleaned since Mrs. Carter's death, and while all the furniture had been removed, the original curtains were hanging in every room. I kept discovering pockets of clutter—pots and pans in the back corner of a kitchen cabinet, old clothes hanging in the laundry room.

Each time I came across one of these caches, I had a creepy feeling, as if I'd just run my fingers through cobwebs. I finally settled down to a systematic scouring of the house, and after I'd removed what was left of the Carters' belongings, the place began to feel as if it were truly ours. But it wasn't ours after all. We were sharing the house with a reluctant Mrs. Carter.

It had to be her. Mrs. Carter was the only other woman to have lived in this house. That meant I was hearing the voice of someone who had died seven years before.

◆ ◆ ◆

I LOOKED FORWARD to talking over this experience with Tom. Between us, we'd be able to figure out what to do. At the very least, I would have an ally. It wouldn't be just me against Mrs. Carter.

"You're not going to believe what happened today," I said as soon as he walked through the door. I was right about this. Tom was shocked, but not for the same reasons I had been.

When I finally paused for breath, he cut into my narrative with "You think you heard *what*!" It wasn't a question. Tom isn't the kind of person who loses his temper easily—he abhors friction of any kind—and so, while I hadn't thought about what his response might be, I was surprised by his rage. Rage not at the thought that he was living in a haunted house but at me, personally, for suggesting that such a thing might be possible. How could I! How could I *think* it—I, his wife—when no reasonable person would entertain the possibility that a ghost even existed, let alone speak to it! It was in my mind. Obviously. All of it. And he didn't want to hear another word about it.

I often bowed to what I saw as Tom's superior intellect, his ease of articulation, his gift of argument. Initially, that night I found myself reverting to form, wishing I hadn't heard Mrs. Carter. No doubt my life would have been easier if I hadn't. Thinking it over later, I knew I had heard her—or had heard something—and I couldn't pretend I hadn't. Tom's winning our argument didn't make him right. He was a lawyer, after all; he was *trained* in argument.

I went to bed that night feeling I was worse off than I had been earlier. It wasn't just me against Mrs. Carter; now it was also me against Tom. The next day I took my story to a more sympathetic audience.

◆ ◆ ◆

ROLFING IS A kind of bodywork that reaches deep into the bones. It has nothing whatsoever to do with spirit communication, yet I felt that someone involved in the healing arts might give this ghost story a hearing. With her lip liner, her manicured hair, and back issues of *Cosmopolitan* on her coffee table, this Rolfer wasn't my idea of a classic healer. Her touch, however, was magic, and so I took the risk of telling her about Mrs. Carter. I was relieved when she wasn't startled.

"This kind of thing does happen," she said, "more often than people think. People who die when they're very old have often gotten weaker and weaker over time. It all happens so slowly that, when they finally cross the line and the body closes down, they don't know they've died. They don't realize that anything has happened."

She added that because they don't see the guides who come to take them to the next plane, these unfortunate souls are trapped here. "It can be very confusing for them. There are people," she said, "*kind* people, who take it upon themselves to work with the souls who don't know their body is gone. These people explain to the lost souls what has happened to them.

They tell them to look for their guides."

"Where are they supposed to look?" I asked.

"The guides are there. They're always there."

She sounded certain. And the process seemed pretty straightforward. This was something I could do for Mrs. Carter. I'd always thought of myself as a kind person. I could be one of these midwives of death. I'd just be giving Mrs. Carter information—information she clearly needed.

The next afternoon, as soon as I got home from work, I sat down to meditate in the room where I'd heard what I was now calling The Voice. I went into the same posture, started the same slow breathing, and within a few minutes the same quavering voice was there: *Get out of my house!*

I took another deep breath and began addressing this entity in my mind: *Mrs. Carter, my husband and I bought this house from your children.* This was such an odd thing to be communicating. How could she not know this? I hadn't planned what I would say, and I regretted not having given it some forethought. But I soldiered on, forming the words in my mind as slowly and clearly as I could.

Actually, you're dead. This was the wrong approach. I could feel it.

You died a few years ago. Also wrong; maybe worse. I tried a new tack.

I know this must be confusing for you, but it's time for you to go on now. You need to look for the guides to take you on to the next place. This sounded hopeful.

There was a moment of silence. The voice came back, louder than before: *Dead! I'm not dead. You're trying to kill me.* And then, stronger in volume and power than anything said so far: *I AM GOING TO KILL YOU!*

I opened my eyes wide. This was not going as I'd hoped. Where were those damned guides?

This time I did leave the house, walking straight out the back sliding doors, across our covered deck, and around to the right side of the house, where, under the deck, I stored my garden tools. Crouched there beside the deck, pulling out a trowel, I felt a chill, a visceral wave of fear, pass through my body. The voice had gotten my full attention, but this was more than just words; this was a moment of tangible threat. I looked up; a huge hanging basket was directly overhead. I jumped back.

My herb and vegetable garden lay at the back of the yard, and that was where I spent the next several hours—far away from the house. I didn't go inside until Tom got home, after seven. His being there was a comfort, although I didn't dare tell him what had happened.

As I went to sleep that night, in some corner of my mind I heard maniacal laughter. Was I creating this drama? This was happening in my mind, certainly, but was it happening *only* in my mind? Was Tom right? Why would I do this to myself? I love a good story. Was I giving myself one humdinger of a story?

The next afternoon, watering the houseplants, I got to the basket of impatiens that had been over my head the day before and saw something that chilled me all over again. One of the three wire prongs holding the basket aloft had been pried loose, wrenched from its mooring, and twisted back a full three inches from its original position. This was not my imagination. This was material, it was measurable, and it was recent. The basket had been intact the last time I'd watered, three days earlier.

Since all of this had started with meditation, I called my hatha yoga teacher for a consultation.

"Of course it's real," he said. "There are spirits around us all the time. Most people can't see or hear them, but if you ever do, the thing you should *not* do is try to communicate with them. Don't talk to the dead! That's rule number one."

The normal, waking, workaday world is for the living, Rick told me. The dead aren't supposed to manifest in this world. "The main way spirits have the power to be here," he added, "is when we, the living, pay attention to them. You're the one who gave this Mrs. Carter the power to go after you. Stop talking to her. Forget all about her."

There is a classic meditation story in which a master tells a student he'll be able to meditate as long as he doesn't think about a monkey. Just *try* not to think about a monkey after that! What I did was to stop meditating in the house, and when I heard what seemed like maniacal laughter, I consciously ignored it. I trusted Rick that if I didn't talk to Mrs. Carter, she couldn't touch me. In that I felt safe.

◆ ◆ ◆

THE EXTERNALS OF my life didn't change immediately after my encounters with Mrs. Carter, but I was never again the same. It was as if I had undergone a seismic blast that created minute cracks throughout the structure it would eventually demolish. Up to that point, I had seen life in material terms. I didn't think about this much and spoke of it even less, but I'd held the view that in all probability death was the end of the line. Once you died, that was it. *Fini. Bas. Nada.* No more story.

Following a casual Episcopal childhood (going to church twice a year whether I needed to or not) and an early teen rebellion in which I decided to be rebaptized as a Disciple of Christ, at some point in my late teens I'd said to God, *I'm not taking this on faith any longer. If you exist, that's fine, but you're going to have to show me.*

It seemed a reasonable, even responsible stance, and the longer I went without some kind of psychic appearance or divine utterance to prove otherwise, the more secure I felt in my theological dispassion. I never, however, called myself an atheist. I was aware of being open to the possibility that there might be more going on here than had yet been demonstrated to me. I felt God might still show himself.

Then, in my early twenties, I married Tom, who, following a casual Jewish upbringing, did identify himself as an atheist. For seven years it had seemed as if we lived by the same philosophy, but we didn't, at all. That became clear when I told him about our ghost.

For the first time, I recognized that an impassioned stance against the existence of spirit is, by definition, faith-based. It's not the kind of thing that can be proven. Yet the person who looks at life from that perspective leaves no room for evidence, or even experience, to the contrary.

I, on the other hand, was now fascinated by this new world I had glimpsed—a world in which there are experiences I could perceive but not prove; in which, beyond the material reality I knew, lay a subtle reality. *Of course it's real*, Rick had said.

There was a lot for me to explore.

2. &cy; Talk Story

A FRIEND AT THE PAPER, Toni Withington, and her husband, who was, like my husband, a lawyer, left their busy life in Honolulu and moved to the relative tranquility of Hawi on the Big Island. When they came back for a few days' visit, Tom and I and some other friends met Toni and her husband for dinner at a tiki-torch restaurant in Waikiki.

After the first flurry of settling in at the table, I caught Toni's attention and asked her, "How did you do it?" She had always been ahead of me. She was a year ahead of me at Northwestern, a year ahead of me on the *Star-Bulletin*, a political reporter while I wrote society features, and here she was now, a dropout! While I was slogging away as features editor, Toni was eating papaya on the beaches of the Kohala Coast, free as a hippie.

Puzzled by my question, she asked, "Do you want to move to the Big Island?"

No, not exactly. "I know I want to make changes in my life," I told her. "I have to. But I have no idea how to do it."

Toni smiled. "You won't know until it's time," she said. "Then you'll know. When the time is right, you'll know exactly what to do. And you'll just do it."

This was what I was looking for. Something that said, *This is the change you should make. Now is the time to do it.*

◆ ◆ ◆

THE *HONOLULU STAR-BULLETIN* was written and edited in a cavernous room lined with teletypes and packed with desks.

Along the windows were glassed-in offices for the specialty sections, one of them being features. My desk was just inside the doorway of our office. I greeted all comers and answered the departmental phone. As a management plan this was unwise, but I saw myself as the guardian of the gates, battling the forces of stodgy tradition.

Ours had been a society section, replete with scrapbook items—stories and photos of interest to only the people involved. When I got the job, at age twenty-three, I changed the nature of the stories we ran—from society (certain successful people) to lifestyle (everyone). I felt almost evangelical about this switch in focus. I saw our section as an opportunity to broaden readers' horizons, revolutionize their interests, and tell them the stories of people who'd made nontraditional choices. In the features section, we could write about anything—sensitivity groups, street theater, hippie communes; how to build a kite, live with a mastectomy, make marshmallows . . .

My enthusiasm wavered with time—I couldn't help but see that our groundbreaking stories hadn't noticeably improved the world—and the newspaper's unremitting deadlines began to feel like a menace. I had a dream, repeatedly, in which the press was a huge, hungry dragon. The monster had to be fed a daily quota of stories: entertaining stories, unique and accurate stories, well-written stories, stories of the right length and offered at the right time. I was in terror that my offering would be inadequate or insufficient or, worst of all, late, because then the dragon would surely eat me. I'd wake up from this dream feeling sick with dread, an emotion that was with me, hidden, through most of my waking hours.

◆ ◆ ◆

MY GHOST STORY, which I never even considered recounting in the *Bulletin*, offered me some relief from the pressures of work. I told this story to friends and was surprised when several of them countered with ghost stories of their own—if not experiences they'd had, then stories they'd heard. Hawaiian lore is rich with such stories: sightings of warrior spirits who go on midnight marches through what are now suburban neighborhoods, or encounters with the goddess Pele, who takes the form of an old woman and appears to travelers on a roadside or in the mountains to give them a warning.

Because I was sharing a personal experience that was inexplicable and subtle, I began to have a new feeling about stories. Telling stories became a kind of exploration, a reaching out. In Hawaii there is a phrase that both celebrates the local culture's largely oral tradition and also describes the way Hawaiian people are with one another—*talk story*. In this tradition, to encounter another person, under any circumstance, and walk away with no personal exchange is the height of rudeness. You always take the time to talk story, to share of yourself. It was something I had never done on deadline, something I didn't truly know how to do. I began to learn that I had to talk story, at least with the people I knew.

The big story that was happening in my life was something I never talked about, didn't like to admit even to myself. My marriage wasn't working out.

I had no real reason to complain, and I knew women who did. I had a friend who wore long-sleeved blouses in the tropical sun to hide the bruises she got from her husband, a seemingly mild-mannered executive who flew into periodic violent rages. Another friend was married to a lawyer Tom knew who fondled other women at parties and, his wife told me, showed an alarming interest in their thirteen-year-old daughter. These women had lots to complain about in their husbands.

What was my husband doing? Tom wasn't hostile, or unfaithful, or unkind. He was indifferent. He wasn't paying enough attention to me. This was a pedestrian grievance, one that after seven years of marriage many wives, perhaps most wives, could make. Maybe if we'd had a child, or even a dog . . . Instead we had a cat, one cat, and he was as remote and independent as my husband.

In my waking hours at home, I was usually alone. I left for

work before Tom was up and returned hours before he came home. On a good night he'd be back by seven, but if he was working on a case or writing a brief, it would be eight or even nine, and for him Saturday was also a workday.

I hung out in our comfortable, quiet little house. I did hatha yoga, I gardened, I cooked dinner, sometimes I read . . . Lately I'd taken up weaving on a hand loom I'd built myself with four boards and four huge nails. I made little wall hangings, explorations in wool that Tom asked me not to put up in the living room. "They're nice," he said, "but this is our public space. You can hang anything you want in the bedroom."

It may not sound as if I was giving much energy to our marriage myself, but I thought about it a lot. I found it lonely to share a space with someone who didn't seem to want to be with me. I kept trying to come up with ways to catch his attention: cook the foods he liked, make little drawings on the notes I left for him in the kitchen on some mornings, wear something enticing when he arrived home at night, come up with interesting amusements we could do together on Sundays.

And Tom would often agree to attend a lecture or take a workshop or see a movie or have dinner with another couple. The public and ceremonial parts of our marriage were in place, but what I actually wanted from my husband was a converging of our minds, and there I think I just wasn't as interesting to him as the practice of law.

The one time of day when I could count on talking with Tom was at night, just before bed, when we shared a nightcap. I looked forward to this. I liked talking with my husband, sharing the little events of our day, comparing notes on our reactions. In these conversations sometimes I would lose myself, go into a mental space that was not quite psychedelic but not quite grounded, either. I found it lovely.

Then one day Tom bought us a television, our first, so that we could watch the evening news when he got home from work. When he walked in hugging that big box, I knew I'd been defeated. And since I spent my days in the cacophony of a

On a weekend outing in central Oahu, 1973

newspaper office, televised news was the last thing I wanted to see before going to sleep.

◆ ◆ ◆

ONE OF THE great advantages of my job on the *Bulletin* was that I found out about the best concerts, classes, lectures, workshops, whatever. Tom agreed to come to this workshop, I think, because it was given by friends of ours.

For two days, a couple dozen of us sat around Theo and Mary's living room, going through a series of exercises in which we dropped, one by one, the basic accoutrements of verbal communication. Meaning, gesture, facial expression, tone of voice—all of it went. For what seemed like hours we sat in pairs, asking each other in monotone, "Do fish swim?" or, "Do birds fly?" and responding yes, no, or maybe.

When Sunday evening came, we were paired with the person we had come with and asked to look into their eyes, saying nothing. I was nonplussed by what happened then. For the first time in my life, I could feel my heart opening. I could feel love as a sensation. This subtle, almost liquid feeling began pouring out of my body and, most particularly, out of my eyes. Love was streaming from me into Tom, into his eyes, and from his eyes back into mine. I could feel a bridge of love between us, and that love *was* the communication. It was the only communication that mattered.

I was overcome with wonder. So this was *love*. This was what people meant when they talked of loving or being in love. Love had only ever been an idea for me: a way of speaking, a tone of voice, a facial expression, a collection of actions, a sort of well-wishing. It had never been a physical experience. Not for me.

This inner event was of a higher order than anything I had ever before felt. How had it happened? All I know is that somehow, after a weekend of ever-narrowing focus, my mind sufficiently quieted to allow me to experience the state that is the goal of meditation practice—not just *meditating* but *being in meditation*.

What I knew even then was that, like The Voice, this experience was real. I don't know of any way I could have proven that, any way my state could have been measured or recorded or verified. But when I walked out of that workshop, my subjective experience was radiant, quite different from when I had walked in. And I carried that radiance with me for at least a week, maybe longer.

Going into the office the next morning, I had a wholly new experience of people I'd known, most of them, for years. This was particularly striking with my assistant, a woman who just the week before had been my personal bête noire. Belinda looked for and often found my weakest points. She was constantly sparring with me, making verbal jabs, pointing out my faults. I knew she wanted my job, or maybe my neck, but on that day I didn't care.

"Good morning," she said, and, looking into her bright blue eyes, I felt nothing but love for this woman. That day I rediscovered her sparkle, her wit, her humor. I remembered why I'd hired her. Was she trying to cut me down? What did it matter! She wasn't hurting me. In this space of the heart, nothing could hurt me. It was as if, having been asleep for the whole of my twenty-eight years, I had awakened and found myself in a celestial realm. This was the kind of story I wanted in my life.

◆ ◆ ◆

THE EFFECT OF the weekend workshop didn't last. My job at the paper expanded; I was given a new section to bring into being, and I put more of myself into that section than I actually had to give. The job had to be done, so I did it the way I'd always done any job, giving it whatever I thought it needed— and losing myself in the process. Though I felt my state slip, I wasn't worried. Tom and I were going on vacation in a month. I'd get it back then.

But I didn't. A two-week vacation is never a panacea, and on this one I spent the first week angry. That week Tom and I were skiing in Vail. (*Vacation* means a change, right? Living in a tropical paradise, we opted for snow.) We went with another couple, and I didn't realize until we got there that the men were planning to ski together and I was expected to stay on the bunny slopes with the other woman, a beginner. I didn't particularly like this woman, but even if I had, I felt shunted off—and insulted! I insisted on skiing with the men, and when Tom pointed out that the runs they'd be tackling were perhaps a bit beyond my current capabilities, I said, "I would rather die than ski on the bunny slope." It was not my finest hour. I skied by myself, and I vividly recall having a miserable time of it.

The second week, Tom and I took a couple of workshops at the Esalen Institute. This was our second visit to this consciousness-raising center on the California coast, and I figured, *Okay, it'll happen here.* The first workshop was over a weekend, and I spent most of that time on the floor, sitting astride a huge pillow. The session leader brought in his girlfriend, along with a sense of being adrift and many of his own burning questions. It seemed as if the weekend was over before we got started, but I felt I was in good company.

The next workshop, which was to be five days, began immediately after, on Sunday evening. The leader, fatigued from his drive from San Francisco, sat in a corner and directed a dozen participants to move around the room, pretending we were animals while he played DJ and changed the music. At his command, we ran, we galloped, we skipped, we crawled, and at times we slithered around the floor on our bellies. Other people were laughing and getting into it, but this wasn't what I wanted to be doing. I played at it, I pretended to do the animal thing, I even smiled, but under it all I was livid. I felt manipulated and frustrated and panicked. This himbo was leading us through a formulaic exercise, and he wasn't showing us the courtesy of participating. How in hell was galloping around like a horse or crawling on my hands and knees like a bear cub going to get me back into a state of unconditional love!

Lying in bed that night, seething, I understood that I didn't have to go back to the workshop. The next morning, I went to the office and found out I could, indeed, just be at Esalen if I chose to. I didn't even have to stay in the room with my husband. "People do it all the time," a woman at the front desk told me. "They get here and find they need the space to think something through."

I could give myself that. The idea of it was thrilling. I carried my suitcase to another room, a woman freed. While Tom was in the workshop, I sat naked and alone in the Esalen baths, looking out over the unfathomable beauty of Big Sur and pondering my life.

◆ ◆ ◆

I HAD SPENT virtually the whole of my twenties trying to tamp down my anger—the same sort of anger I was experiencing on this very vacation. The pattern was that I would put up with something I didn't like—skiing on bunny slopes or pretending to be a python—and then at some point erupt. Explosive volcanic eruptions involve the release of contracted, compressed power and the spewing forth of molten rock. Human anger is nearly that destructive, and when you're the one out of control, it can be horrifying—even if you're just yelling, even if you're just saying mean things to someone. Actually, the eruption itself is quite satisfying; it's dealing with the debris afterward that's a horror. I had gone to countless sensitivity groups and encounter sessions and through five years of psychotherapy so I could *do* something about my anger. If I didn't, I would lose the two things that meant the most to me—my marriage and my job. It was a given.

That day in the Esalen baths, I saw it differently. I'd been working hard, actively trying to live up to what I perceived as the requirements of my life, but what was I receiving in return? The image that came to me was a long gray corridor, like the inside hallway of some grim little hotel, with all the doors closed. I knew I had to start opening those doors. I had no idea what they represented—missed friendships? Limited scope? Stifled expression?—but I did know that the doors were closed because I had sacrificed so much for the sake of my marriage and my job. After serving those two arenas, I had no energy left for anything else. Perhaps it was one reason I was so angry. It was definitely why that luminous experience of inner love had disappeared weeks before. There was no way love could survive in the gray corridor that was now my life. I could no longer wait for a change to come; I needed to take action.

I couldn't just leave my husband. It would be like severing a limb. I would stay with the marriage a little longer, I decided, but the job I would change as soon as I got back. I'd resign my position as section editor. No one would stop me from stepping down, not when someone qualified wanted so very much to step up. I'd go back to being a reporter. I'd be writing, telling the stories myself, putting myself on the line again. That would be good.

Was it what I wanted? I didn't know. But if I didn't make this move, I might never know. So that's what I did.

Changing jobs did not, of course, immediately change my life.

3. ℴ The Flip of a Coin

THE HIGH POINT OF MY WEEK was my hatha yoga class. About eight of us met on Thursday evenings at a local church under the guidance of Rick Bernstein, a dedicated yogi who had changed his diet, his drinking habits, his politics, and his livelihood and, besides all of that, spent several hours every day performing asanas for the love of it.

Asanas are hatha yoga postures and have earthy names like downward-facing dog, cow face, cobra, and pigeon. I had started practicing yoga several years earlier as a way of dealing with what is known in some circles as "editor's neck." Yoga did alleviate my physical symptoms, which mainly involved rock-tight shoulders, but the practice began to do much more than this for me. Yoga became a way of being quiet with myself.

"Let yourself rest in the posture," Rick would say. "This isn't a competition—not even with yourself. Go to the edge of where your body feels comfortable. Stay there." After a few minutes, he'd say, "Now see if your body wants to go a little deeper."

I reveled in this practice. I was long-legged and thin—actually, I'm still long-legged and thin, but at the time I was strong and supple as well. I felt satisfaction just being in a posture, being in any one of maybe twenty of the postures I preferred. I wouldn't say I'd mastered any of them. In yoga, mastery is another level altogether. To master a posture, you have to be able to remain in that posture for three hours with ease. That means without discomfort, without frustration or impatience.

I wasn't even trying for this. But I found I enjoyed being in the postures, and for me that was magnificent. When Tom and I were skiing, I noticed that I felt great only when I got to the bottom of the hill, whereas he felt great all the way down. For me, hatha yoga was like that: I felt great the whole time I was doing it.

This was not, however, enough. Rick told our class that hatha yoga is not an end in itself. There is a point to hatha yoga, he said, and that point is meditation. You do hatha yoga so you can meditate. Hence, the reach of our yoga class extended to include chanting Sanskrit mantras, which we would do for a few minutes before beginning the asanas, and also meditation, which we would do following the corpse pose at the end. Chanting was an activity—we were singing—and I could accept it on that basis alone, but I didn't understand this other pursuit, the thing that was supposed to be the point of hatha yoga.

I would lie flat on my back in the final posture of our class, the corpse pose, my body humming with energy, my mind fairly quiet, when Rick would rouse us by chanting the mantra *om* a few times. We sat up and assumed a cross-legged posture, and at that point my reverie ended. My mind kicked in, and I would sit there for a brief eternity, thinking—half thoughts and phrases shooting through my mind, some person's face appearing with an expression I didn't understand . . . Was something else supposed to be happening? I had the feeling I should be *doing* something. When it was over, I felt disappointed, though when Rick asked how meditation was for us, I invariably said it was nice.

It wasn't terrible; it just wasn't very much. Was something supposed to happen in meditation? I had no idea. I'd had that experience with The Voice while I was trying to meditate. I was pretty sure that hearing voices from the dead wasn't the purpose of meditating, but what was?

One day Tom pointed out to me that often I would look off, unfocused, and murmur, "I don't know." Then,

"I wonder."

"You say that all the time," Tom told me. "*I don't know. I wonder.* What is it you wonder?"

"I don't know," I said. "I wonder."

We both laughed, but I didn't find it especially funny. There was so much I truly did not know. And I *was* wondering. By now I had made that shift from section editor to reporter as a leap of faith. I was watching for some sign that it was the right move, that I was headed someplace I wanted to end up being. What was coming before my screen was confusing. The most satisfying part of my life was the practice of yoga, and if yoga was only a preparation for meditation, then what was this meditation? There is a lot of confusing information around about the practice and state of meditation, and I encountered it frontally, with no way to discern what was a natural part of the process, what was unrelated, what was a direct result, what was something that *might* happen but was best avoided . . . I didn't know. And I did wonder.

◆ ◆ ◆

ONE NIGHT AT the end of yoga class, my experience of meditation was marked and astonishing. I closed my eyes and took in a breath, and the top of my head came off. It felt to me as if a cap that formed the top of my scalp was lifted from my body. In my mind's eye, I looked up and peered out of the new opening in my head. It seemed that some force was looking down, looking *in* at me, and beckoning me. This wasn't anything I actually saw; it was a feeling, an intuition, that some disembodied force was inviting me—or some level of awareness I thought of as "me"—to step out of my body. I considered the possibility. But, no, I didn't want to take this step. A step into what? The force seemed to reach in toward me, then urge me, actually trying to pull me out. At that I hunkered down. I rooted my awareness into my tailbone, into the earth itself, and hung on as if my life depended on it. At the moment, it seemed that it did.

After a timeless space, the force was gone. I opened my eyes and found others in our circle opening their eyes, too.

Rick said, "I got the definite impression someone was hanging out with us tonight." I was surprised, but I didn't say anything. After a pause, he said, "I spent this afternoon with Swami . . . ," and then he mentioned a name. He went on to say that this swami, who was a monk and a teacher, was in Hawaii for just one day and would be back in a few months' time.

"I think he came to see us tonight." Rick was smiling now. "He didn't want to wait."

I could wait. That was one swami I never wanted to see. Not ever.

◆ ◆ ◆

I HAD DECIDED to write a beginners' guide to meditation. This is, as any feature writer knows, an excellent way to learn more about a subject that interests you—do some research and write about it. It wasn't going to be an esoteric piece. I wanted to write about meditation in a simple way, so that people could read it with their morning coffee, put the paper down, and try it themselves—a recipe for meditation.

I spent about an hour and a half interviewing Rick Bernstein, and he gave me exactly what I was looking for: directions on how to sit (back straight), how to breathe (deeply and slowly), where to put your attention (on the breath itself), and why you might want to do this (a sense of peace ultimately comes). I went back to the office and wrote it up in less time than I'd taken talking to him.

A few days later, he called at the office. "Peggy, you know that interview we did on meditation? Don't do the article. It's not right."

I was annoyed. Was he going to be difficult? "What do you mean it's not right? It's perfect." I added what for me was the clincher: "I've already written it."

"*Please* don't print it." His voice carried an unusual intensity; Rick was normally Mr. Cool.

"What's this all about?"

"I'm not an expert on meditation," he said.

"What are you talking about? You've been teaching us meditation for months. What you said about it was perfect. You were completely clear."

"Just because we've been meditating a little in our class doesn't make me a meditation teacher," he said. "Look, there's a master of meditation coming here very soon. Put that article aside, and I'll get you an interview with him."

In my experience, a feature in the hand is worth ten promised interviews. Besides, I was sure this meditation master would say pretty much what Rick had said, just not as clearly. But Rick was a friend, and a friend's peace of mind is no small thing.

So I agreed to interview this visiting master of meditation, a swami—*the* swami, I understood—and Rick set it up for me.

◆ ◆ ◆

A FEW WEEKS later, Jocelyn Fujii, another of the *Bulletin's* feature reporters, asked if I had time to talk with her. There was no space for private conversation in the office, so we went to the newspaper's coffee-and-juice bar. The garden café was a bleak spot—metal chairs, Formica tables, a few desultory potted ficus, a view of the parking lot—but it was convenient, relatively private, and, except at noon, never crowded.

As soon as we sat down, Jocelyn got to the point: she'd heard I had an interview set up with this swami.

Oh. So that was it. I'd worked with Joce (pronounced *Joss*) for about five years. I was her first editor, her first boss right after her graduation. She was bright, a quick study, a good writer. She was a local girl from an established Japanese family on Kauai. As section editor, I'd encouraged the feature reporters to write about subjects that fit their interests. One visited communes on Maui. Another committed herself for a time to the state mental institution. Jocelyn went on a week's fast, and she was often the one who wrote about yoga. The only problem was that now I was a writer again myself, and the topics Joce enjoyed exploring were my own interests.

Jocelyn went on to say that she'd been setting up the interview with the swami through another route. Basically, my contact got to the swami's people before hers did. As gently as she possibly could, she said, "I am the person who usually does this kind of interview."

She was indeed. Not only that, this was the very swami I had told myself I never wanted to see. Yet, inexplicably, I did want to do this interview. Anyway, I felt right about doing it. I told Joce about my exploration of meditation and how this swami seemed to be the perfect way for me to do an article I'd been working on for quite some time.

"We never set up the features section so that anybody actually had a beat," I said. "It's not as if you were covering the courts and I showed up at a trial." With features, there would always be some overlap, and when there was, it seemed to me the first person on a story should be the one to do it.

"There are other ways of looking at this," Jocelyn said. She, too, had a particular interest in this story, and hers dated even further back than mine. The swami's last hosts in Honolulu, the people whose house he'd stayed in on a visit four years earlier, were two of her closest friends. For four years now they had been saying they'd get her an interview with the swami when he came back. For four years she had been looking forward to talking with him.

We went back and forth like this—point, counterpoint— for a full hour and a half. We moved from the swami and this particular article to a discussion of every previously unaired issue that had come up between us in our five years of working together as editor and writer. We said things like, "I never understood why . . ." and, "What were you thinking when . . ." and, "The way I saw it was . . ." To give us credit, there was never a raised voice or an impolite word, never a suggestion that this was anything other than a congenial sharing of perspectives between friends.

After we'd talked everything out, however, our original dispute was still a draw. I saw that I couldn't say, *I got this interview first; it's mine*, and I also couldn't say, *Joce, it's fine; you take it.* Then it came to me: "We'll flip a coin."

Jocelyn laughed. For both of us, it was the perfect way. We'd defended our positions, heard each other out, and now we could leave the answer to destiny, to the fates, to pure chance. I wouldn't have been able to articulate what the deciding force or factor was, but I knew I trusted it.

One of us came up with a quarter, she called, I tossed, and it flew. That silver disc went high in the air, hit the table, danced for a moment, and rolled off to the floor. Joce and I got down on our hands and knees, laughing, and found the quarter was still rolling.

"That swami is looking at us right now and laughing," she said.

I won. But you knew that.

4. ☙ The Swami's Advance Man

I GOT A CALL AT THE OFFICE from a man who said he was with the swami's organization. He wanted to prepare me for the interview, he said, and to see what we could do to let people in Hawaii know the swami was coming. The swami would be on a tight schedule—three days in Honolulu ending with a big evening event at a venue in Waikiki; a retreat on Oahu's windward coast, and then another on Maui. It was little more than a week in all, and if the public didn't find out about his visit until the day after he arrived, the swami would be gone before most people even noticed.

That was reasonable. For me this was a how-to-meditate article; for the swami it was publicity. I told the man to bring by a press release and I'd make sure it got in the paper.

I thought the swami's advance man would wear white; I thought he'd be calm, ethereal, and, above all, yogic—which to me meant physically trim, flexible, fit, and focused on maintaining a superlative level of health. The body-is-a-temple idea personified.

Ron Morrison didn't fit the picture on any level. He looked like the middle-aged entrepreneur–world traveler he was. He had a paunch, Prince Valiant hair, and big black-lensed glasses that almost hid the bags under his eyes. Leaving his dark glasses on, he introduced himself at my desk.

"Is there anywhere around here we can get coffee?" he asked, and at the garden café, he got not just the coffee but also a huge, doughy sweet roll. "Breakfast," he said.

Breakfast? It was eleven o'clock. What kind of yogi was this?

◆ ◆ ◆

I ASKED MORRISON how he'd hooked up with the swami, and he told me a story that took me with him, along with his wife and their one-year-old son, on a journey to three continents, to five or six countries, and into the presence of two holy men. The family arrived first at the ashram of the other of these holy men—not our swami—and on his birthday.

"It's considered good to be around these guys on their birthday," he said. "It's like Christ and Christmas."

"So we get to India, and there are seventy-five thousand Indians celebrating this guy's birthday. That is instant India. We're in the country there; it's rural and it's rough. We have a tent with us, but there are no shelters, there are no bathrooms, it is steaming hot . . ."

He wasn't complaining. I could hear in his voice that Morrison was perfectly happy about all of this and had been at the time. How could that be?

"You see this guy, and you swoon. He shows up, everybody swoons, and we swoon, too. It may have been mass hysteria, but it's what was happening."

My pencil was sprinting across the pad. The writer in me wanted to get his words down—this man was so funny, so unstudied in his responses—while at the same time the reporter in me was trying to take in what he was saying. The moment he paused, I sent out a volley of questions: "But this isn't your swami. How does your swami fit into this? Your press release says he's a saint, and it sounds like this other guy is, too. Why do there seem to be so many saints in India?"

He started with the last question. "There are different holy men to reach different people. What turns me on might not turn you on.

"Like, when I saw the first holy man, even though I felt love, I instantly knew he wasn't my guru. When I saw Swamiji,

I had the same experience of love, and, besides that, something clicked for me. I knew, *This is the one.*"

◆ ◆ ◆

WHY HAD MORRISON decided to go to India? He said the first step was selling his real estate firm in New York and moving to the West Coast to become a potter. He divorced, remarried, had a child, and was living a sweeter, simpler existence in Carmel on the Monterey coast. "It was good," he said, "but it wasn't enough."

I knew what he meant.

Ron Morrison had been living in Carmel about three years when Ram Dass came through on his way back from his first trip to India. Morrison had known Ram Dass back in what he referred to as "the Timothy Leary days." This was when Ram Dass was Harvard professor Richard Alpert and was experimenting with Leary to turn the world on to the consciousness-expanding possibilities of a new psychedelic drug, LSD.

"So, in Carmel I go to this talk Ram Dass is giving, and the message I get is very strong: India is where it's happening. The man I'm seeing is different—he is completely different— from the man I knew just a few years before. Ram Dass is glowing. He is radiant. He is full of light. And it has nothing to do with drugs."

Those were the terms Morrison used to describe the swami as well, except instead of talking about the swami's state, Morrison talked about the way a person feels in the swami's presence.

"When you're with him," he said, "just being there, you beam."

But how could this be? How does the swami do it?

"He doesn't use any techniques. What he uses is where you're not, and he flashes it at you like an enormous sun. If you put up a lot of resistance, it burns you. But if you flow with it, the amount of joy that comes is indescribable."

The explanation didn't actually make sense to me, but I knew

I was feeling pretty good talking with just the swami's advance man. He was talking and smiling; I was taking notes and smiling. I guess you could say we were both beaming.

"Yeah," Morrison said, "you've gotten a little buzz from this. Just wait till you meet him!"

◆ ◆ ◆

AS I LISTENED to Ron Morrison go through his story, it occurred to me that here, sitting before me, was a man who had undergone a personal transformation.

I'd heard the word *transformation* defined just a few weeks earlier by the consciousness-raising entrepreneur Werner Erhard in an introductory program he gave in the Ilikai Hotel ballroom for an upcoming event of his organization, known as est. Yes, the lowercase is correct; it was a play on the Latin *to be*, as well as an acronym for Erhard Seminars Training. Enlightenment in two weekends was the promise the graduates, if not the organization, made for this event. It sounded ridiculous, but I was intrigued by Erhard's charisma, his eloquence, and his mental acuity. Even though I was covering the intro for the paper, after his talk Tom and I signed up to take the est seminar, which was happening in about a month.

That evening Erhard had said *transformation* is a change not in the way you act but in the reasons behind your actions. Once you're transformed, your motives change. I'd been wondering about that ever since, curious about what real transformation would look like in a person's life. Talking with Morrison, I got a glimpse of it.

Morrison was a hustler. He was as persuasive and fast-talking as any New York realtor, so he was probably acting the same as he ever had. What was different was the reason for his actions. He was no longer motivated by the desire for money. He was donating his time and energy, along with his one-liners and his dry wit, to help this swami. Morrison was supporting himself and his family on his investments.

"Oh, am I losing money," he laughed. He seemed not to care. His motive, as he described it, was the outpouring of love he experienced when he was in this swami's presence.

◆ ◆ ◆

I HAD TO convince the swami's advance man to let the *Star-Bulletin* take his photograph. "Just a mug shot," I told him. "It's nothing."

"You don't understand," he kept saying. "This isn't about me. You should run *his* picture."

What I understood was that if I had only the swami's photo to offer, the *Bulletin* would run a one-column mug shot with the bare bones of his press release and nothing more. But with Morrison's smiling face, the newspaper ran my interview—thirty-six column inches—under the headline "The Man Who Can Make a Swami Appear." As publicity goes, it was pretty good.

Actually, Morrison was right, as I later found out. He wasn't supposed to be the topic of our discussion. He got flak about the article and about the two-column photo of himself that ran with it. Not from the swami, I think, but from others on the swami's staff who saw the article. Months later, one of these women said to me, "The ego of that Ron Morrison. So offensive! Putting himself forward to the press like it was all about him."

"That was me," I said. "It was my idea. Ron tried to tell me not to do it. He said I didn't understand. I insisted . . ."

I had insisted. It's the sort of person I was. Am.

Just as Morrison was a hustler in his service of the swami, I—someone who could be adamant about her own point of view—had my own distinct qualities to bring to my meeting with the holy man.

◆ ◆ ◆

IN THE WEEK after my interview with Morrison, I went through a ritual that was becoming routine: the diet. I had become seriously invested in being slim. Both Tom and I had a terror that I would become like one of our mothers—plump, bosomy, overbearing women. I was overbearing at times, but at least I wouldn't be plump. I was nearly five ten, and I never wanted to weigh more than 130 pounds. As soon as I reached this upper limit, I would diet by whatever means appealed to me—the water-protein diet, the water-vegetable diet, the grape diet—until I again was down to 120. I did this two, maybe three times a year.

When I say the diets appealed to me, I don't mean to imply that I enjoyed them. On these diets, no matter what I was eating or how much, or how much I had liked those foods when I began the diet, by the end I craved whatever I was denying myself. Usually I went off the diets with relief and as soon as I felt I could.

This time, however, when I reached my goal, it occurred to me that if I kept on with the diet a little longer, I would weigh less than 120 when I began eating normally and would therefore be able to wait longer before dieting again. Tom wasn't home for dinner at all that week, so the regime was easy to maintain; there was no other food to tempt me. Then one night at the dining table, I looked at the undressed salad on my plate—lettuce, tomatoes, cucumber, green onions: the foods I was allowing myself—and felt a moment of unease. I wasn't *feeding* myself, and for just a moment, I was struck by the wrongness of it. Then I remembered my reason: *Now I won't have to diet again for a long time.*

I picked up my fork and continued the diet, making the choice I considered self-disciplined. I didn't know that it heralded something else entirely.

◆ ◆ ◆

THE MORNING I was to interview the swami, I sat at home, fidgeting. His plane wasn't coming in until noon, and that gave me the whole morning to . . . to what? Prepare? There was no need to prepare. I had only one question to ask him: *please tell me how to meditate.* I knew what I wanted to ask him, and I knew what I wanted him to say. I had, in fact, already written the story. What I needed from the swami was for him to confirm it.

So why was I nervous?

For one thing, I couldn't figure out what to do with this unexpected gift of morning time. I couldn't garden, because I'd get dirty. I couldn't talk to anybody, because everyone I knew was at the office, working. I couldn't read, because I wasn't sure what I *should* read before meeting a swami. I certainly didn't want to read anything that might agitate me.

One thing I was certain of: I wanted to be calm. A swami would be calm, so when I spoke with him, I should be calm. And I didn't want to be late. When I have a long wait for something much anticipated, one of the dangers is that, to pass the time, I'll get wrapped up in something unimportant and thereby miss the main event. Or if I didn't miss the interview altogether, I might find myself running late and becoming agitated. *More* agitated. Even more agitated than I already was.

At ten I decided to leave for the airport, which was about a half-hour drive from my home. I would stop at Ala Moana Park on the way to commune with nature, sit under a tree, gaze at the ocean—the ideal preface to my interview with the swami.

Once I got to Ala Moana, however, I wondered why I'd imagined I would be more comfortable in a public park than I was in my own home. First was the question of how to sit on the grass in peach linen pants without staining them. I found a straw beach mat in the trunk of my car and, and, putting this mat under a large, flowering poinciana, I sat facing the ocean. It may have made a peaceful picture: a young woman sitting in dappled shade under brilliant yellow flowers, apparently gazing at the sparkling ocean. But in that moment I didn't feel peace; I felt breathless anticipation.

Years later, seeing Niagara Falls, I found myself mesmerized by the tranquil approach of the river to that intense, vertical leap—a leap of greater length and velocity than any other on the continent, a leap that changes the very nature of the river.

Not that it becomes something other than water, but the water becomes an altogether different kind of force. I watched the Niagara River's serene approach to the falls as if hypnotized by the image, until finally I recognized it as a symbol for an experience in my own life: my meeting with the swami.

Unlike the river, I knew something was coming; I just didn't know what.

As I got up to leave the park, I discovered that a phalanx of ants had joined me on the beach mat. For a moment I froze. Wasn't there some injunction in India about insects? I didn't want to do violence here. I picked up a leaf and used it to urge the ants—invite them, really—to return to the grass. I folded the mat with the feeling I had just encountered a test.

I wondered what I was walking into with this interview. I didn't know what would be asked of me or what was at stake.

5. ⌕ "I'm Not Speaking to a Child"

ON MY WAY INTO THE AIRPORT, without prior thought, I swung the car into the drive for the lei sellers' stalls. In Hawaii it's a tradition to greet visitors with flower garlands, but it wasn't a tradition for reporters going into interviews, and I'd had no conscious thought of doing so with this swami. Once I was there, however, I figured I might as well follow the custom. I bought a plumeria lei, cheap but cheerful, with fragrant yellow and white flowers.

With the lei over my left arm, I walked into the VIP lounge, where the interview was to take place. Uh-oh—why was there a crowd here? Most of my interviews were one-on-one. I had pictured myself talking with the swami and a translator in a tête-à-tête on one of the plush white couches in a corner of the room, but that wasn't going to happen. There were easily fifty people milling around in here. Notepad in hand, I approached a woman I'd seen at a recent workshop I'd taken.

"I've never met a swami before," I told her. "I'm a little nervous. What's he like?"

"I have no idea," she said. "I'm meeting him for the first time myself."

Going from person to person, I found that almost everyone I talked with had never seen the swami before. They'd heard of him through est or Arica (another consciousness-raising group) or from a yoga teacher or because they knew someone who'd met him years ago.

Yet when this mystery swami finally walked into the room with a traveling party of about twenty-five, there was no doubt which of them he was. In the flurry of "He's coming," "He's here," "Oh, it's him," I saw a short, wiry man moving through the room like a wind. He was wearing a red shirt, a purple vest, a saffron lavalava, red socks (no shoes), dark glasses, and a bright red stocking cap. But it wasn't just the clothes. The swami moved like a force of nature, and he glowed.

◆ ◆ ◆

IN A MOMENT of focused hubbub while potted palms and chairs were moved, people found places to sit. A woman in an orange sari, standing at my elbow, leaned over and said in my ear, "You can give it to him now."

I looked down at the lei, then across the room, some twenty-five feet away, where the swami sat alone on a couch. I took a breath and walked over to him. Once I was close enough for a good look at his face, I paused, not sure if I should proceed. His eyes were closed. I figured the guy was probably exhausted. He was in his midsixties, he'd gotten off a five-hour flight with probably some hoopla at the other end, and he was headed into an interview. Here I was, about to interrupt his one quiet moment.

As I started to turn and tiptoe away, the swami opened his eyes and smiled at me. It was as if the sun had just come out; my whole body felt that smile. It was a smile that took me in and accepted me, appreciated me, let me know I was in the perfect place at the perfect time and doing the perfect thing. The swami motioned me forward. As I arced the string of plumerias above his head to put it on him, he caught hold of my hands and moved them back, so that we both put the garland on me instead.

Then he smiled at me again and closed his eyes.

I had never had a more economical exchange with any human being. Not one word was spoken, not an extra gesture made. At the end we were exactly as we had been at the beginning, maybe five seconds before, except that the lei, instead of being in my hands, was resting on my shoulders.

As I walked away, I considered how this swami didn't play to anyone's expectations. He hadn't been concerned about what I thought he should do or how I took in what he did or how it might look to anyone watching. He did what he knew needed doing. I wanted to be like that.

It was a gift, that glimpse of freedom.

◆ ◆ ◆

MORE SPECTATORS KEPT arriving in the room; there were a hundred people there, and I started worrying again. How was I going to get the swami to relax and speak naturally with so many people watching?

It wasn't the swami, of course, who needed to relax. I had a terror of public speaking. The last time I'd tried it, seven years before, I'd fainted at the end of my talk and had to be carried offstage on a stretcher. The prospect of being put forward as a part of today's entertainment was dreadful. I was used to one-on-one interviews in which asking dumb questions could elicit brilliant responses. Who wanted to ask dumb questions with so many people watching!

Also, another reporter had shown up: Patricia Hunter, from the other daily paper. Not only had Pat won two national awards for feature writing, she had the jump on time. She'd be able to get her story in the next morning's paper, while mine wouldn't be out until that afternoon. It doesn't sound like much, and it wasn't, but the thought that what Pat wrote would be both first and likely better was added intimidation.

Someone led me back to the swami's couch, where the majority leader of the Hawaii State Senate was being introduced to him. The governor was supposed to be there, but he was ill, the senator was saying. Could the swami meet with the governor at another time?

I was taking notes on this exchange, when someone indicated two chairs next to the swami, where Pat Hunter and I were to sit for the interview. The translator and our audience would be on the floor, watching us.

"If everyone else is on the floor," I said, "that's where I'm sitting." It may have seemed as if I had enormous respect for the swami, but that wasn't it. I had no idea how I would handle this interview, and I thought people would be more forgiving if they saw me on the same level they were on. Also, I wouldn't be quite so exposed.

◆ ◆ ◆

PAT SAID I could begin, and in a small voice I asked, "Would the swami please give me instructions on how to meditate?"

The answer was immediate and surprisingly short: "If you want to meditate, spend time with someone who meditates, and it will happen spontaneously. You will begin meditating."

Wait a minute. What about posture? What about breathing? What was he talking about, anyway?

"I'm sorry," I said to the translator, "but he must not have understood my question. I want to write a beginners' guide to meditation, something that teaches meditation to people who know nothing about it. Could you explain that to the swami?"

Looking pained, the translator turned back to the swami. He spoke in Hindi for a few moments, and the swami smiled. Once again, he said something very short. As he got to the end, a few people in the audience laughed. The translator turned back to me and said, word for word, the same thing: "If you want to meditate, spend time with someone who meditates, and it will happen spontaneously. You will begin meditating."

The translator was smiling, a lot of people were laughing, and I was flummoxed. I didn't understand what the swami was saying. It sounded like nonsense to me. I considered asking him about my own experiences of meditating—the night the top of my head disappeared or the threats from Mrs. Carter—but these I ruled out as inappropriate. How could I ask about visitations from subtle entities—one of whom might have been the swami himself! I certainly couldn't write about such things in the article.

As I pondered, the silence stretched to an uncomfortable

length. At last, Pat Hunter stepped in with some reportorial questions: "How long will the swami be here? Does the swami have a message for the people of Hawaii?"

As the swami answered and a back-and-forth was established, I was feeling one-down. Then I heard the swami say something that I knew was wrong. He said that in meditation people could go into hatha yoga postures spontaneously.

At that point I'd been practicing hatha yoga for five years and had been meditating once a week for six months. I was in a position to know that these were two entirely different disciplines. Not only had this man refused to give me coherent meditation instructions, now—worse!—he was putting out misinformation. Did he expect me to write this up, put it in the paper, and make a fool of myself?

I glared at him. "Really," I said.

"Yes," the swami said, "really." Then he said, "I'm not speaking to a child. I'm speaking to a newspaper reporter, and I know what I'm talking about."

◆ ◆ ◆

THERE ARE MOMENTS in life when you perceive a choice. That's what this was for me. I could flash back with something else—God only knows what I would have said—or I could take in what this monk, who had been described as a living saint, was telling me. I chose the latter course.

I took a breath, and with that I could feel the swami's *I'm not speaking to a child* come into me like a depth charge. The words hit my solar plexus and came deeper, ever deeper, until there was something like a detonation in the area of my heart. I had a vivid image of myself as a four-year-old girl with a notepad on my knee, pretending to be a newspaper reporter. He *was* speaking to a child.

He laughed, and with his laugh something tight in me loosened. I understood that the swami didn't mind my being a child. In fact, he liked the child. He hadn't been taking aim at me. What he didn't like was my pretense. I could just stop pretending.

I let go of the notion that I should turn in the story I'd already written. I assumed that I was talking to the swami because he had something to say, and I began asking him the questions that came up for me.

"What is the difference between Eastern and Western religion?"

The swami said there is no essential difference. How could there be? Your ocean is as salty as the ocean in our country, he said. The air has the same oxygen. It is the same sky here as it is there. The sun from which you get your light is the same sun as the one from which we get light.

But what about the matter of gurus? There are so many around now. How can a person tell which of them is real and which is not?

The swami said that, unfortunately, there is no instrument by which you can distinguish a true yogi from a phony one. Only by spending time with him, by following his teachings, can you tell who is real and who is pretending. You know from your own inner experience. If you evolve—if you become a stronger, more joyful person, he explained—you're with the right one.

At one point I tried to look closely at the swami's face, but he was sitting with his back to a bank of windows and was silhouetted against the light. As I looked up at him, the air around him danced in a kaleidoscope of shifting forms. I shook my head and returned to my notepad. This was an interview. I needed to focus.

Pat and I were invited to join the swami's party for lunch at the place where he would be staying that week. We both declined, saying we had to get back to write our articles. As I turned to go, the swami asked if he'd be seeing me again.

"Oh, yes," I said. Until that point I hadn't thought about seeing him again, but in that instant I knew I would.

◆ ◆ ◆

AS I SET out to find my car, I realized something had happened to my mind in the course of the interview. From agitated and tense, I had become euphoric. I couldn't remember where I had parked, and, unaccountably, I didn't care. A couple who'd watched the interview were in the same situation, and the three of us giggled like teenagers while we searched the parking lot—not usually one of my favorite entertainments. Once I was finally in the car and on my way back to the office, I realized with a start that I was driving down Nimitz Highway singing, in full voice, the chorus from "Oklahoma." Well, why not?

Back in the office, I flipped through my notebook and found I could decipher only occasional words. I felt like I was looking at hieroglyphs, notes from centuries before recorded by someone who not only spoke another language but used another alphabet as well. I panicked. I had nothing to write! I didn't even know if I could describe the swami. I felt like I'd hardly seen him.

I did have the address of the swami's house. I decided to accept the invitation to lunch. I drove well over the speed limit but not so fast that I'd get stopped—and this time I wasn't singing.

The swami was staying in a white-frame bungalow on a prestigious beach. A rock walkway cut across a meticulously tended lawn to a set of stairs and shaded front porch piled with hundreds of shoes. Taking off your shoes before you enter a house is a Japanese custom. It's common in Hawaii to find shoes at the front door, but rarely so many as this. I stepped out of my shoes, thinking I might never see them again.

The room had a vaulted ceiling and a bank of windows overlooking the ocean. The swami sat cross-legged in a huge chair, the only chair, which was placed in front of a black stone fireplace. He was facing both the view and the crowd. The room was packed with people. I sank to the floor where I was, just in front of the door.

Everyone was chanting—sounding like and yet unlike anything I'd ever heard in yoga class. The main difference was the volume. With so many people singing, and singing full-voice, the room vibrated with sound. I couldn't make out the words, but I could hear that it was call-and-response, led by the swami, who was holding a huge tambourine in his lap. The moment I sat down, the swami made rapid staccato slaps on his tambourine. Saying something about it being time for lunch, he handed off the instrument and left the room.

I wouldn't have the chant to write about, but I needed something. I'd go for crowd color. I was looking around for someone to speak with, when I felt a tap on my shoulder.

"You're here," the translator said. "How nice. Do you have more questions for the swami?"

"Uh-h. Yes. Sure."

I was ushered into a small room where a handful of people waited—a few Western women in orange saris and men in long white Indian shirts. These followers of the swami sat on the floor, facing a large chair. I joined them there. In a moment the swami walked in and sat down, smiling at me, and the translator—this time an older Indian woman—said, "What are your questions for the swami?"

It was another moment of truth. I didn't have any questions for the swami. I just needed a spark of something that would allow me to write about the experience of meeting him. But I couldn't say that, and once again a silence was developing. I just jumped in with the truth.

"I came because I couldn't really see you at the airport. There was so much light. . . ."

The translator spoke as I spoke, and before I'd finished, the swami started laughing. He had a rich, deep, infectious laugh that came from somewhere deep inside his body. He reached over and began to flick my forehead with his fingers, back and forth, gently and at the same time forcefully.

"He's giving you a blessing," the translator said. "He's giving you *shakti*."

This gave me something to write about.

You Expect Lightning at Least

Laughing, the swami reached over and flicked his fingers against my face, back and forth between my eyes.

"He's giving you a blessing," his translator said.
"He's giving you shakti."

I waited for lightning to strike or cannons to roar or something to signify that I had gotten the divine grace I have heard people describe in relation to this swami. . . . Instead what I felt was my contact lens popping out of my eye.

Oh lord, I thought. What now?

A few moments later, five of us were on our hands and knees, patting and stroking the thick green carpet, looking for the small plastic disc, while the swami sat in his chair and asked his translator what we were doing and how he could have done that.

Someone came up with a flashlight, and I came up with the lens. The swami looked it over carefully, blessed it, and said he wanted one, too.

He was like that. A delightful man, perfectly natural and very much at ease in what could have been an uncomfortable situation with a strange reporter and a strange form of eyeglass . . .

After we'd talked about the lens for a few minutes, the swami told someone to take me outside, to give me lunch. He said that I needed to eat something. From my perspective, I was in a state of bliss. I could feel love radiating from my heart in waves. It wasn't that I loved the swami; it was just that I felt love, nonrelational love.

I barely noticed the food, except that it was excellent and vegetarian. We ate under a huge, branching tree someone told me was a Bodhi tree, from a cutting of the original Bodhi tree under which the Buddha had become enlightened.

When I got back to the office, the article poured out of me like warm honey. I didn't write about being a four-year-old or about the Bodhi tree or about the feeling of love—which I was no longer experiencing by the time I was sitting at my typewriter—but I put in pretty much everything else, ending with the swami's Honolulu schedule.

As I finished writing, I saw another possibility to be with the swami. He was holding open meditation at the house where he was staying for the next three mornings, beginning at five thirty. It was the perfect time, since I had to be at the office at seven. I would be able to find out whether spending time with "someone who meditates" would improve my meditation.

I planned to attend his lecture in Waikiki Thursday evening with Tom, but we weren't taking his meditation retreat over the weekend. I'd set up dinner engagements for Friday, Saturday, and Sunday just to be sure I wouldn't be swept away by this swami. I was still wary of him. But only just.

6. ⌒ Try Again

THAT NIGHT I HAD TROUBLE FALLING ASLEEP, and through the early hours of the morning, in anticipation of meditating with the swami, I kept waking up: one o'clock, two, three . . . I didn't want to be late, but this was ridiculous. Finally, at four, I got up and dressed.

I'd mentioned where I was going to Tom, but this was nothing new from his perspective. I was always up earlier than he in the mornings. This was just quite a bit earlier.

Arriving at the swami's house in the predawn light, I noticed that the pile of shoes on the porch was smaller, more orderly, than it had been the day before. I slipped off my sandals, making a point of putting them at the edge, where I'd be able to find them again easily. Getting to work on time was going to mean scrambling a bit at the end.

I pushed open the screen door and found the room dark and silent. There was a strong scent of something sweet in the air, and the only light was from two candles, placed on tables on either side of the chair the swami had sat in the day before. This morning the chair was empty. I was disappointed, but as long as I was there, I might as well stay for meditation.

I stood at the doorway for a moment while my eyes adjusted to the dim light. The room was again filled with people, but this morning it was a looser fit—fifty people, instead of a hundred. Sitting in any cross-legged posture takes space, however, so people were by necessity spread out. I found a spot where I could just barely fold my legs into position without touching the three people closest to me. I had to fit myself into place like a puzzle piece, facing a side of the room instead of the front. The "front" was clearly the swami's chair. Directionally, I was out of sync with the people around me, but it was the best I could do.

Almost as soon as I settled, everyone began chanting in a foreign tongue—Sanskrit, I presumed, though it wasn't the kind of Sanskrit chanting with which I was familiar. The chanting I'd done had been call-and-response in a simple, rhythmic manner that's easy to pick up if you're willing to try. This was something with verses, and even when the refrain came up, it was so complex I couldn't make out the sounds clearly enough to echo them. I didn't feel responsible even to try for the meaning.

Everyone *else* was singing, and some part of me felt I should be singing, too. But how? I hadn't been given the words. I didn't know them. Why had I been put in this position? It was unwelcoming. It was rude. Finally, by the seventh time the refrain came around, I was able to jump in and sound a few of the words, but my triumph was short-lived. The song ended almost immediately, and another began. This was a back-and-forth chant, but once again I had never heard the words before, and once again they were too complicated for me to catch in progress. This was followed by another, simpler chant, but by now I was finished with singing. I hadn't gotten up at four o'clock in the morning and driven halfway across the island so I could sing. I had come to meditate. Were we never going to meditate?

◆ ◆ ◆

WE DID MEDITATE. The singing stopped, and there was silence in the room as we meditated—for an hour. My meditations had been five or ten minutes. I had never before tried to meditate for an hour. I had never sat cross-legged for an hour. And I had certainly never sat for that length of time on a bare wooden floor, wedged between three people in such a way that it was impossible for me to move without disturbing one of them.

My knees began to ache. I had never known pain like that—sharp, shooting pains so intense that I thought if I couldn't move my legs, I might scream. But would screaming help? I didn't see how. And if I didn't want to disturb the people next to me by moving, why would I scream?

For that interminable hour, I sat. I made no sound. My mind, however, was anything but quiet: *What am I doing here? Why did I come? I could be in bed. I could be sleeping. This is ridiculous. It's torture! God, my* knees! *Will this never end? Will I be able to walk?*

It was not a pleasant journey, but by the end one thing was clear: I was finished with meditation. When a bell finally rang, indicating the session had ended, I congratulated myself on surviving an ordeal. I pulled my legs into my chest in preparation to leave, which I planned to do just as soon as I could stand without falling. I was already rising, plotting my route over outstretched legs and around supine trunks (whose heads were lowered to the floor), when I heard a small gasp in the other direction. I looked around and saw that the swami had come into the room. He was just then sitting down in his chair.

Out of respect, I resumed my seat on the floor.

The swami turned to an open-faced young woman who was sitting just to his right. He smiled and began tapping a spot just between his eyebrows, looking at her with a question in his face, as if he were asking, *Did it happen?* The woman gave him a beatific smile and nodded.

The swami turned to a young man leaning against the wall on the opposite side of the room, his eyes closed. The swami spoke to his translator, and the translator called across the room to the young man, "The swami has a question for you."

Someone next to the man tapped him on the shoulder, and once his eyes were open, the translator said, "The swami is asking if you enjoyed meditation."

The man laughed. He never said anything, and he didn't stop laughing.

Finally, the swami said something else, and I heard the

translator tell the person next to the man, "You should take him outside now. He needs to eat something. Give him a couple of bananas."

Bananas?

As he was led from the room, the man was still laughing.

The swami turned then to me. He didn't smile. He didn't speak. He didn't make a gesture. He just looked directly at me, and I found myself saying, in my mind, *Okay. I'll come back. I'll try again*. Because by that time it was obvious to me that even though meditation hadn't worked for me, it was working for some people. It was worth it to me to try again.

A half hour later, I walked into the *Star-Bulletin*'s ground-floor entrance, stopping at a stall in a cubby between the parking lot entrance and a back stairway leading to the editorial offices. I picked up a packet of nuts from the shelves and smiled at the vendor. "Good morning," I said to him.

He looked at me with surprise. Surely I'd spoken to him before. "It is a good morning," he said, and he smiled, too, a beautiful smile. Because of an affliction, he had to hold one hand with the other to make the change, and it took some time. Was this why I usually didn't buy anything from him? Was this why, in the seven years we'd both worked in this building, I'd never had a conversation with this man? Because I found his infirmity awkward? But he was lovely. He was radiant. I knew in that moment he always had been.

"I hope the rest of the day is like this," I said.

"I think it will be," he said.

And it was. Perhaps *this* was one benefit of spending time with someone who meditated.

◆ ◆ ◆

I WENT FOR meditation again Thursday morning. Once again, it was a long hour, but not nearly as painful as the day before. I arrived early enough to secure a seat by the wall. That meant I could lean back. It meant I wasn't surrounded on all sides. It meant when my legs began hurting, I could move them. The wall did not, however, do anything to quiet my mind. Afterward, the swami didn't come in, and I was relieved. I wouldn't have had any experience to report to him if he had.

That night, Tom and I went to hear the swami's talk at the Waikiki Shell. As we walked from the car, Tom sang, "Swa-a-me-e-e, how-I-love-ya-how-I-love-ya . . ."

I laughed even though I didn't find it especially funny. It felt like we were thirteen again: one friend was making fun of another, and I didn't have the courage to stand up for the one who wasn't there. I didn't want either of them to know how I felt about the other. I didn't want Tom to know how fascinated I was by this swami, and I didn't want the swami, or any of his people, to know that I'd just laughed when someone made light of him.

The truth is, I wasn't a part of either world. I was feeling estranged from my husband, but I wasn't feeling at one with the swami, either. That night, Tom and I sat in the huge amphitheater with many hundreds of other people, listening to the swami's stories from Indian scripture, singing a Sanskrit phrase again and again in tune with a hand-pumped organ, smelling the sweet incense . . . It was foreign, every bit of it. I had a vision that another kind of life than the one I was currently leading was possible, but I wasn't at ease with the swami's world and I had no compelling reason to step into it.

◆ ◆ ◆

I WENT TO meditation the next morning almost as a matter of form. It was Friday, the last day the swami would be in Honolulu, and I was following through on something I'd agreed with myself that I would do. Then, in the last moments of meditation, I looked into the inner darkness that was all I could see and it seemed to take on a texture, almost like velvet. I looked at this black velvet more closely, giving it my full attention. When I did that, it seemed to become a curtain, like a stage curtain—which then opened. It pulled back to reveal a luminous disc, like a huge, radiant sun the color of light golden honey. This disk of energy radiated warmth—not physical warmth but a subtle warmth, like love. Just looking at it, I could feel love. I knew intuitively it was a deeper part of myself—of *me!*—than I had ever before experienced.

It was like a miracle. I had spent the last five and a half years exploring various forms of self-discovery. I had thought that everyone else in the world operated by an inner radar that I alone lacked. I always looked around myself for verification and cues. This vision of inner light was, for me, like finding a treasure. This luminous disk was the inner identity I'd been seeking all that time. I was sure of it.

The meditation bell rang, and I rooted my awareness in the radiant inner orb. I had no intention of leaving it, not when I had just now seen it! This was exactly the kind of experience I'd been thirsting to have. It was of the same order as the experience I'd had months before, with my heart, but this was somehow even greater because I could *see* it. And now that I had it, I wasn't going anywhere. . . .

I had my focus on that vision when a fly landed on my arm, jarring me, and I was suddenly thrust back to my normal consciousness. Just before I opened my eyes, I heard a voice inside say, *You have work to do.*

Whoever or whatever that voice was, I knew that *work* didn't mean the newspaper. Before I left the swami's house that morning, I signed up for his meditation retreat. The retreat was opening that night, but it would be fine for me to arrive first thing on Saturday morning. I had no idea how I was going to do it, but I knew this was where I would spend my weekend.

◆ ◆ ◆

I WENT INTO the *Star-Bulletin* that morning, but my real focus was on getting myself to the retreat. I called Tom to let him know. I made another call, to cancel our Saturday-night plans. "This is your idea," Tom had said. "You call it off."

On my lunch hour, I found a sporting-goods store and bought a sleeping bag to be my bedding for the next two days.

We had guests over for dinner that night, so I went to bed late, but I was up by three the next morning and pulling out of the driveway within half an hour. I was determined to make it to the retreat—maybe an hour's drive away—in time for meditation at five. I wanted to bask again in that inner light. Now, at last, I knew what meditation was.

Or so I thought.

7. ✑ Eleven Hours of Chanting

THE SKY WAS JUST BEGINNING to lighten when I pulled into the retreat site, a flower farm on Oahu's windward coast. Leaving my things in the car, I set off in the predawn twilight to find the meditation hall. It turned out to be a huge tent.

I slipped in through the main entrance, which was at the back. It was dark inside. Some candles burned at the front, and after a moment I could make out that people were sitting in informal rows, with an aisle in the middle to the swami's chair at the far end of the tent. I couldn't see if he was there.

Finding a spot near the back, I arranged my legs in the cross-legged position I found most comfortable, the half lotus. I started breathing slowly, deep breaths in and out, scanning my inner field for that inner sun. What I was looking at seemed to be the backs of my eyelids—no radiance there. I realized that my shoulders were gently rotating, and I stilled them. Where was the light? Almost immediately my shoulders were moving again, and this time I changed position and purposefully lengthened my back to keep my body stationary. What was happening with my shoulders?

A fragment from the swami's interview wafted through my mind: *whatever comes up in meditation is sacred; you shouldn't fight it; just let it happen.*

Uh-oh. Maybe I'd just squelched something. Would that movement in my shoulders come again? I hoped so.

It did, moments later, and this time when my shoulders

shook, I let go of motor control. As before, the movement started gently, almost imperceptibly, and when it wasn't stopped, it grew—in velocity, range, and effect. Within a few minutes, the trunk of my body was moving in huge circles and my shoulders were shimmying like a dancer's. It's as though someone had me by the shoulders and was—this was the phrase that went through my mind—shaking the shit out of me! My body vibrated like a thing possessed.

I wasn't terrified. I felt quite peaceful. I was watching it all happen from a safe space inside myself. I was sitting in the eye of my own personal hurricane, untouched by the storm raging around me in my body. As I watched, the action altered and, instead of originating in the shoulders, the movement became centered inside my chest—actually, in my lungs.

My body continued to vibrate, but now it was subtler; it was coming from my breath. I was breathing in-and-out-and-in-and-out-and-in-and-out in a rapid-fire succession that was, I finally recognized, bellows breathing, *bhastrika pranayama*. I had been trying to perform this classic yogic breathing exercise for the past four months in hatha yoga class and had been unable get my lungs to cooperate for more than a moment or two at a time. Now I was doing full *bhastrika pranayama*—and doing it spontaneously, while in meditation!

Yes, the swami knew what he was talking about. If I had any lingering doubts about what he'd said in the interview, they were being laid to rest right now as my natural bellows breath went on and on and on, without effort, without even volition on my part. All I was doing was watching it happen.

◆ ◆ ◆

MY INNER STORM subsided. The meditation session had ended. That was when I got my first inkling of why this astonishing meditation might have occurred. As I stood up, I could feel that the muscles in my shoulders were loose and relaxed. I mentioned that the original impetus to my hatha yoga practice had been the editor's bane: tight shoulders. Now I felt as though twenty pounds of tension had fallen from my torso. My shoulders were loose and relaxed. I was so buoyant I couldn't stop smiling. As I moved to the entrance of the tent, I noticed that walking was a new experience. Walking felt wonderful!

Later, I learned *bhastrika pranayama* also cleanses the lungs— the lungs I had filled with tobacco smoke day after day from my midteens to my midtwenties. This, too, was a benefit that came from my active meditation.

As I left the tent, the sun had just risen. Retreat participants were being served breakfast cafeteria-style, then taking their food to straw mats set out on the lawn. About fifty were there, and I recognized a number of them. Most of Rick's hatha yoga students had come, as well as Jocelyn Fujii and another reporter and a few other people I'd met at weekend workshops along the way. One woman introduced herself and said she was there because of my article on the swami. "It's going to be an interesting weekend," I told her. "That much we know for sure."

The food was served on plastic trays with compartments, and in plastic bowls and drinking glasses. Breakfast was fruit, hot cereal, and Indian spiced chai. I was perfectly happy. I was happy with everything. I looked up from my tray and asked, "What happens next?"

Rick, sitting beside me, gave me a dour look. "Eleven hours of chanting," he said.

I laughed. Surely we wouldn't be doing that!

◆ ◆ ◆

BACK IN THE meditation hall, we began chanting. First we sang a *namasankirtana*. That's pronounced *NAH-muh-sun-KEER-tun-uh*; it's the call-and-response singing of mantric phrases. This sort of chanting is easy, and—if you get into it, if you actually *sing*—there can be an immediate and perceptible payoff. It can open the heart. I didn't notice anything that morning.

Following the *namasankirtana*, we sang a Sanskrit hymn of twelve verses.

Following the hymn, we sang what struck me as a dirge, though I now know that is not what it is. We were doing a kind of singing called *svadhyaya*, pronounced *svuhd-hee-AI-yuh*. This is the chanting of a Sanskrit text. When we got to verse 28, I began flipping through the photocopied chanting book to see how much more there was: a lot of pages—181 verses! This must be what Rick had meant.

In looking ahead, I lost my place in the chant, but that didn't matter. Trying to find the right place again gave me something to do. I couldn't sing a word. I wasn't even attempting it.

When we arrived at verse 181, I put down the chant book with a sense of real gratitude. I couldn't take another minute of it. I was wrong. I could. And I did. A moment later everyone was standing to sing yet another hymn, and after that we sat again for a final *namasankirtana*.

In all, it was an hour and a half of Sanskrit chanting. Not quite eleven hours, but that's what it felt like to me.

◆ ◆ ◆

THE DAY BECAME heavenly. The swami had been there for the chant, and now he spoke. Almost as soon as he began speaking, I entered a sort of trance. You could say I was asleep. I looked as if I were asleep—sitting cross-legged as I was and bent forward, arms on the floor, cradling my head—but when I finally sat up again, I wasn't sluggish in the way I usually am when I first awaken. I felt alert. I felt wonderful, as if I'd been meditating.

During the lunch break, I did asanas on the lawn. I know this because years later someone showed me photos he'd taken of me in various poses: the warrior (standing, arms and legs outstretched), the shoulder stand (legs lifted straight up in the air), the plow (legs curled up and over my torso, my ass pointed skyward). I was mortified to see what a spectacle I had made of myself, and what I was wearing!

To this meditation retreat with an Indian saint, I had chosen to wear what I thought of as spiritual clothes: short shorts; a long-sleeved, almost sheer, white cotton blouse with strategically placed embroidery; and no bra. I had noticed that women around the swami were dressed in saris, swathed in cloth from neck to ankle, but in my mind that had nothing to do with me. I was demonstrating that I knew the appropriate attire for a weekend workshop in Hawaii.

Following Indian custom, men and women sat on opposite sides of the tent: women to the swami's right, men to his left. The swami was asked about this practice in a question-and-answer session in the afternoon. People wrote their questions on slips of paper and submitted them to be read aloud. The wording of this question was confrontational: "Why do you find it necessary to keep men and women apart at this retreat?"

The swami spoke about how we had come together this weekend to meditate, to experience something profound within ourselves. He gave a disarming smile and asked: Is it necessary to be touching each other all the time? Can't you let go of each other for just a weekend? When the retreat is over, you can be together again as much as you like.

◆ ◆ ◆

I WAS MOST interested in what the swami had to say regarding *kundalini shakti*, an inner energy whose awakening I knew I was experiencing. The term *kundalini* means "coiled one," a reference to the shape of the subtle channel in which the energy, when dormant, is locked. This channel is located at the base of the spine, roughly at the center of the physical body. Not that this energy is in the physical body. You couldn't cut open your spine and find your *kundalini* any more than you could cut open your brain and find your thoughts.

Kundalini awakening was the swami's specialty. *Kundalini* is a subtle force, he said, and it operates in what he called the subtle body. Once released, *kundalini* undertakes the work of cleansing on all levels—physical, mental, spiritual—so that the individual can ultimately become a clear channel, for this energy, for God.

I was wary of the G-word, but I recognized that I was taking in what the swami offered only bit by bit, as I was able. He had spoken about *kundalini* during the interview and in his public talk, but because I'd had no previous experience of *kundalini*, I hadn't heard a word he'd said about it.

Now I was hearing it. The spontaneous movements in my meditation that morning were what the swami called *kriyas* and were, he said, a sign that an awakening had taken place, that physical cleansing was happening. Knowing this, I was hungry to learn more. Now, when I heard the swami speak about *kundalini*, I felt I was receiving firsthand knowledge about the secrets of the universe. He seemed to know a lot about subjects I'd never heard of before. Perhaps he had it right about God as well.

◆ ◆ ◆

AS THE DAY warmed, the sides of the tent were lifted, so, while sitting in the shade, we still enjoyed Hawaii's blessed trade winds and could see the stretch of brilliant green lawn on which the tent was standing. Most of the floor was covered with thick carpets, some in vivid Indian patterns. In the afternoon, hall monitors sprinkled the carpets—and anyone who happened to be sitting on them—with French perfume, flashes of pure fragrance. I loved it.

Another custom I loved was the swami's open-handed way of passing out chocolates. People would offer him huge boxes of chocolates, which the swami himself didn't eat. He knew, however, that the people around him enjoyed chocolate enormously, so when he received it, which was almost every day, he had aides pass chocolates to everyone there. I thought he must want us to know that spiritual work could be sweet on every level.

The primary experience of being at that retreat had nothing to do with the sweets, the perfume, or even the words being spoken. It had to do, as Ron Morrison had tried to explain to me weeks earlier, with the atmosphere around the swami himself. In fact, most of the time when he spoke, I went into a space of unadulterated bliss. I could hear his words, but the sounds I heard were coming up from inside me, illuminating layers of my mind I hadn't been aware of. That was one reason I took in those words with such a sense of certainty. They had to be true; they were coming up from inside me!

The swami spoke about this a bit, how the state of the guru is contagious. But he claimed none of it for himself. He'd point to the huge photograph of his own guru that hung above his chair. A partially clothed, big-bellied man with piercing eyes looked down at us from the photo. He's the one doing this, the swami said; it's all his play.

◆ ◆ ◆

THAT NIGHT, there was an eleven-hour chant. The swami described it as an opportunity. Anyone who wished to could stay up all night chanting—chanting and dancing! This extended dancing chant started at seven in the evening and continued until six the next morning: eleven hours exactly.

I didn't begin with the idea that I would be up all night. I was concerned about the dancing part. I'd always been shy about dancing, and this seemed so public. Musicians gathered in a circle, sitting around a flame in a brass holder that was set up in the middle of the tent. The rest of us formed a circle around the musicians. Everyone was facing the flame.

A woman considered the high priestess of ancient hula, Iolani Luahini, had come to dance for the swami that afternoon. She stayed for the dancing chant. Initially, I was entranced by her fluid gestures as she moved around the circle, but after a while, it was the chanting itself that caught me. We were singing *Hare Ram Hare Krishna*, a chant I associated at the time with street beggars. It is, however, an ancient mantra, and its power was palpable that night.

I felt like I had just fallen in love. The love was a felt force, an experience, moving in and around my body even as my body was moving around the circle. I didn't care if I was graceful, on the right foot, or in the right rhythm. The love itself was moving my body. I danced and chanted, almost without break, for the entire eleven hours.

The next morning, I realized that I hadn't washed my face, combed my hair, touched up my lipstick or eyeliner since long before dawn the day before. I had to look like a wreck! I ran into the sleeping tent, where I'd left my overnight bag. I pulled out a mirror and gaped in astonishment. I hardly recognized myself. My face was shining with light. I looked quite wonderful.

It may sound like a small thing, but to me it was monumental. I could actually *see* the love on my face—and there is more beauty in love than in cosmetics.

◆ ◆ ◆

AT BREAKFAST SUNDAY morning the translator asked whether I would like to have a private meeting with the swami. "I could arrange that," he said, "if you have something to ask the swami."

It seemed an honor; I wasn't about to decline. I said yes, I did have a question for the swami.

The translator smiled and said he'd let me know when our meeting would be. "Probably this morning," he said. A couple of hours later, he led me to a small tented area behind the place where the swami usually sat.

There were just the three of us. I could have asked the swami anything. I could have asked him about the spontaneous movements in my meditation, or whether I would attain enlightenment in this lifetime, or if I would accrue bad karma by stepping away from a failing marriage—all pressing questions at this point in my life. I chose to ask about the ghost in my house. I said that I'd been meditating and a dead person had spoken to me. . . .

As I explained my question, the swami shot a look at the translator that clearly said, *You didn't vet this one!* The translator shot back a look that said, *Sorry!*

The swami told me that this kind of thing happens. It was nothing to worry about. I should pay no attention to spirits.

I had the feeling he knew I'd already heard this advice—don't talk to the dead—and felt I was milking the experience to show him that I had subtle awareness. Perhaps I was. I left our meeting with the sense that I'd missed a cue, that something had been expected of me and I hadn't delivered. I had no idea what it might be.

◆ ◆ ◆

THAT AFTERNOON THERE was a sharing session in which participants were invited to talk about their experiences. One after another, people stood to speak about the potentially life-changing inner events of their weekend. I'd been astonished by my meditations—the involuntary movements had continued each time I sat for meditation—and by the sense of physical freedom I felt afterward. I could have spoken about that. But listening to the visions of light, the manifestations of subtle inner music, the profound understandings that had come to the people around me, I began to feel as if what had happened to me wasn't worth mentioning.

One woman said that in her meditations she had been visited by three goddesses—Lakshmi, Sarasvati, and Kali—appearing in all their multiarmed and bejeweled glory and each bearing a personal message for her. "I am so grateful," this woman said. "I had no idea that such divinity was within me."

I would have liked to see goddesses. I thought about this at length during the break that followed, huddled alone on the grass on the beach side of a small bluff. I'd had physical movements, the *kriyas*, and that was something. But it meant I had physical impurities. Here I was, someone who needed cleansing, surrounded by people who were visited by goddesses, people who got personal messages from celestial beings. I sat watching the sun on the water, thinking it would have been such a beautiful weekend if only I'd had some visions. It would have been perfect, if only . . .

I caught myself. I had never had visions of goddesses before. Why should I have them now? This *was* a beautiful weekend, just the way it was. It was splendid. It was enthralling, astonishing, extraordinary! It was sensational! It was beyond anything I had experienced before or ever thought possible!

I laughed at how ridiculous my mind was. Laughed at how silly I was to envy that woman's visions of goddesses. Laughed at the sheer beauty of this moment. Leaning back into the grass, I let my body heave with laughter.

When I peered over the bluff, I saw that everyone had gone back into the tent. It was time for the swami to speak, and I was going to walk in late.

Late is something I never like to be. At the newspaper, *late* meant missing a deadline—and *deadline* meant exactly that: a line beyond which a person was dead. The term comes from German prisoner-of-war camps in World War I: the commandant would draw a line in the dirt, and anyone who stepped across it was shot. The dead line. They never shot anyone at the *Star-Bulletin*, but if you were late, someone had to cover for you, and if you were late on something important, everyone after you in production had to work faster and harder because you hadn't measured up.

The very possibility of being late was enough to make my belly feel tight. To be late in front of everyone, walking in like a bad example . . .

Again I caught myself. Why was I doing this to myself? I had been involved in a perfectly legitimate contemplation, through which I had come to a place of equanimity. What better way for me to spend my time at this retreat? I wasn't late for anything. I was in perfect time.

With that awareness, I walked back to the tent and stepped in through the entrance at the rear. The swami paused in his talk and looked at me. I bobbed my head at him, the briefest of bows, and smiled, and he smiled broadly in return. He resumed speaking. He was talking about how we're all divine beings, how divinity lives right inside each one of us.

In that moment, I could feel it.

◆ ◆ ◆

I'D PLANNED TO leave the retreat midafternoon on Sunday to be back in time for that final dinner I'd set up for the weekend.

I called Tom. He was irritated, but I told him I couldn't do it, couldn't leave early. There was a five o'clock session in the tent, the evening *arati* chant, and then dinner. After dinner, I'd drive home.

Hardly anyone was in the tent at five o'clock. Most other people at the retreat, it seemed, had left about the time I'd originally planned to. Fine. I'd get a seat up front.

I positioned myself in the first row, anticipating that the swami would soon take his seat only yards away from where I was sitting. Instead, one of his traveling party, a South Indian man who was also a monk, stepped up to the microphone. Then I remembered. This man had spoken the previous afternoon at this time. His topic was one of the verses of the Sanskrit text that was chanted in the morning. "Today, we're looking at verse number . . ." He had a nasal, singsong voice cultivated to reach high registers usually not possible for males after puberty. Yesterday, after I had recovered from my initial urge to laugh, listening to this monk had put me into a state of utter torpor. And here I was again, sitting right in front of him. There was no escape.

I took a deep breath—and as the monk spoke, rather than hearing his voice as a parody of teaching, I felt I was listening to the cadenced delivery of pure spiritual wisdom. There's a fairy tale I heard as a child in which a princess speaks words of such profound beauty that as they leave her lips, the words become gemstones—diamonds, rubies, emeralds—and at her feet, the ground is strewn with their sparkling radiance. I remembered that image as this man spoke.

The robe he was wearing—orange cotton—began to shimmer in iridescent colors, one on top of the other. I had never seen such cloth. The walls of the tent—canvas—suddenly looked as if they had been woven from peacock feathers, and like the robe, they were iridescent in the light.

As I drank this in, I realized I was staring wide-eyed around me, my mouth gaping in disbelief. I closed my mouth, hooded my eyes, and looked at the faces of the people beside me. Either they saw this all the time, or I was having this vision on my own. I listened attentively to the monk. It was timeless wisdom coming from him, and I didn't want to miss one word. He wasn't speaking any differently than he had the day before, but somehow I had the ears to hear him now. It was a gift.

I knew it wasn't the monk's power that was making this happen. Probably it was the swami. If it wasn't the swami, it was *kundalini*. And if it wasn't *kundalini*, it was God.

◆ ◆ ◆

WHEN I GOT HOME that night, I told Tom, "I saw God." In the strictest sense it wasn't true. What I'd seen was possibly a sign of God. Or a sign there was much more in the universe than I had ever before thought possible. In the same sense, I'd *heard* God as well. It happened on the drive home that evening.

I'd given some other retreat participants a lift into town. We'd been on the road for a few minutes when I began to hear what sounded like an angelic choir. I said something about the beautiful music on the radio. "What music?" the man next to me asked. "The radio isn't on." Once again, the experience was just for me. The unearthly singing went on and on, with harmonies so subtle I could barely take them in. I was ecstatic for the entire drive. The swami had said that divinity existed within each human being, that to experience it, we needed to turn inside ourselves. What made me know that this experience was authentic, that it was *me*, was that as I listened to this music, I felt at home with it and I felt truly happy.

The bliss stayed with me. At home, one of the first things Tom said to me was, "You look beatific."

"There's a retreat on Maui this week," I told him. "I'd really like to go."

Tom looked perplexed and pained. "Then you should go."

8. ∾ If You Have a Question

I GOT INTO A RENTAL CAR at Kahului Airport and realized I had no idea what to do next. Usually when I was in unfamiliar territory, which Maui was for me, I was with Tom, who always had in hand the appropriate guidebooks, maps, and directions. If Tom had been with me now, he would have known exactly where we were going and would have been in this moment starting to drive us there.

Now I was in the driver's seat, and I didn't even have a map of the island. I'd leaped into this trip without making any effort to prepare for it. I took a deep breath, and it came to me that I did know the name of the school and that this school was in Makawao. I started the car, followed the signs out of the airport, and headed upland toward Makawao. Road signs got me there, all the way to the school.

Perhaps this hadn't been a mistake after all.

◆ ◆ ◆

THE RETREAT'S FIRST event was a lecture the swami gave that evening in a chapel, a little stone building with old wooden pews and lovely stained-glass windows. The swami sat up by the pulpit, and the audience sat in every nook in the sanctuary. People filled not just the pews but also the floor space, all the way up the aisle. Since this was Maui, it was a colorful crowd: hippies or flower children, as they were called, dressed in bell-bottom jeans and Indian prints with a minimum of undergarments and a maximum of beads, feathers, and whimsical hats. On Maui it was more than a costume. On Maui the hippies were tilling the land, sleeping on beaches, living close to nature—and to their own nature. With this particular audience, the swami found exceptional rapport.

He gave a remarkable lecture. First we chanted; then the swami sat in silence for an unusual length of time, maybe five minutes. Finally he said that his mind was silent, that no words were coming. Since there was nothing to say, we'd meditate. After a small spate of knowing laughter, absolute silence followed. It lasted more than an hour.

The following afternoon, with no fanfare and without my having even hoped that such a thing was possible, Tom arrived. He wanted to see what this was, he said. If the swami's world was so important to me, he wanted to give it a chance. I was thrilled, but I had misgivings as well. Tom came at the end of the day, after the sessions in which the swami and others had given talks and answered questions, explaining some of the underpinnings of what was happening at the retreat. He came just before the start of another all-night dancing chant of *Hare Ram Hare Krishna*—which, just as I had, Tom associated with wild-eyed street solicitors who were offering for sale an unwanted *Bhagavad Gita*, which is to Hindus a sort of bible.

The Maui retreat had fewer participants than the one on Oahu, so the swami invited the public to join this all-night revel. The flower children of Maui turned out in full force, approaching the event as if it were a primeval fertility rite, dancing with abandon around the central flame. It seemed as if all the energies of the universe and the denizens of several lower realms had come together to make the night repugnant for Tom. The next morning, the Jewish lawyer watched his wife perform a full-body prostration before an Indian man holding a wand of peacock feathers.

"This is not my path," Tom told me at breakfast. He wasn't curt, but he was definite. He left.

I stayed. I didn't feel that comfortable with the Maui flower children myself, but I knew this wasn't the swami's milieu. Something was happening for me on another level, and I was willing to suspend my judgment on the outer details in order to explore it further.

That day in meditation, I had a vision in which the swami was sitting in his chair and the retreat participants sat in informal rows, facing him. My eyes were closed, but I could see the image of all of us sitting there in my inner vision as if the scene were projected onto the backs of my eyelids. Each of us had a lantern, instead of a torso. The swami's lantern blazed with enough light to illumine the entire room and beyond. Those of us sitting before him had lights as well, but the glass in our lanterns was blackened with what looked like soot. As I watched this curious scene, I saw that the blackened glass was being cleaned by the lights—both the light that each of us carried inside and also by the light that the swami was shining on us.

I toyed with that image in my mind, looking at it from inside myself, looking at it from the swami's perspective. Finally, it came to me: this was purification. It was a metaphor for the very process I was experiencing. Somehow, having an image for it helped me take it all in. I started to think about what would happen once the swami left Hawaii. How would I keep up this cleansing on my own?

◆ ◆ ◆

I BEGAN TO notice the swami's staff. Some were, like the swami himself, from India; others were American, or Danish, or Australian. Except for the swami, everyone spoke English. Talking to various people, I learned that the next stop on the swami's itinerary would be Colorado. I wondered what it would be like to go along.

I posed that question to a young woman from Atlanta who said she had been with the swami in India. "Oh, it's great," she said. "But it's different for everyone. You'd have to find out what it would be for you." She laughed then, and her laughter was infectious, but her words sounded a touch ominous. I didn't know what to make of them—or what I should do.

In his talk that afternoon, the swami said that if you have a question that's bothering you, you should close your eyes and ask it inside. "The answer will be there," he said.

In that moment, I closed my eyes and asked, *Should I follow the swami to Colorado?*

The answer was there. I heard it loud and clear: *Yes!*

The swami had paused in his talk. As I opened my eyes, I looked straight into his. He was watching me. He smiled and went back to his talk.

◆ ◆ ◆

THAT NIGHT I had a new roommate, one of the women from the swami's staff. She had an ample body, a casually pinned bun, a sharp and inquisitive face. She had once been a legal secretary, lived in New York, knew Andy Warhol. I asked her what it was like to travel with the swami.

"It's heaven," she said. "It's the way you always thought life should be. Living with an omniscient being means there is perfect justice. There's no reason to hide or pretend, because he knows everything. Nothing goes on that he doesn't know about. Around him, people always receive what they deserve. It's as if he were everywhere.

"In fact," she added, "I think he may be with us right now."

The swami *was* with us. I could feel it. I was experiencing a level of ecstasy that I had never known—that I *could* never before have known. It seemed as if the swami wasn't just with us in the room but in my very body. I could feel a subtle force inside me that *wasn't* me. It was the feeling equivalent of being infused by perfect light.

"You're right," I said. "He is here." I smiled and turned away from her, to relish what I felt was a rare and beautiful moment. That intuition was correct. It never happened in quite that way again.

♦ ♦ ♦

WHEN PACKING FOR MAUI, I had brought along my most recent weaving. This was a wall hanging, about half a foot wide and two feet long—like me, tall and thin. It was a depiction of the rising sun, but I'd done it in earth tones, in brown and beige and rust. I wasn't especially proud of this weaving, but the urge to take it with me to Maui would not be denied. On the final morning of the retreat, something told me to take the wall hanging with me when I went to the meditation hall.

That morning, I was the first one there. I sat in what I figured would be the geographic center of the women's section and went into an unconscious state. When I came out of it, a number of other people were sitting around me, meditating. The swami was in his chair.

The weaving had become wrapped around one of my feet. As I began to disentangle myself from it, an inner voice told me, *Give it to him now.* From any rational perspective, it was the wrong time to do that. Everyone in the room, the swami included, was meditating. I closed my eyes, and the voice came again: *Now!*

I stood and walked down the aisle to the swami's chair. When I reached him, I paused, not knowing what to do. The translator started to rise and reach for me, saying in an angry hiss, "You can't do—"

The swami shushed him and gestured me forward. I knelt in front of him and handed him my indifferent wall hanging, which he admired, smiling, running the fingers of one hand through the fringe as he held it up with the other. I sat before him, weeping, not understanding why, but knowing that I felt as though I myself had been offered to the swami—and had been found worthy. As he handed the wall hanging back, he articulated, and initiated me with, a mantra. He waved me back to my seat.

I had offered myself to the swami in the form of this wall hanging, and, having admired my offering, he'd blessed it and given it back. Through the rest of the meditation, I wept tears of release.

AT BREAKFAST the translator approached me. Before he could say anything, I told him, "I want to join the swami's tour. I want to go to Colorado."

"What about your husband?" he asked.

I equivocated for a moment and then told him that Tom and I were having problems. "This won't be what ends our marriage," I said. "I think it's only a matter of time."

"You'll have to ask the swami," he said. "It's up to him. Come to the airport. There will be an opportunity, right before we get on the plane. Watch me. I'll tell you when to come forward."

I packed and followed the swami's cavalcade to Kahului and the airport—no need for directions now—returned my car, and sat in a gazebo in the airport garden, my suitcase beside me and the wall hanging clutched in one hand. That, as it turned out, was a mistake.

When the translator motioned me forward, I walked up to the swami, still carrying the wall hanging. His mobile face froze the moment he saw it. He gave me a look that said, *Are you going to wave that like a flag for the rest of your life?*

I had no place to go but forward. I scrunched my bit of woven art into a ball and said, "Swamiji, I want to join your staff. I'd like to follow you to Colorado. Is that all right?"

He nodded. He didn't smile. But I knew it was all right.

◆ ◆ ◆

I HAD MET THE SWAMI just a week before. Later, people would ask me, just like I'd asked Toni Withington, "How could you do that? How could you leave your life and go off like that on a moment's notice?"

With what was on offer? How could I *not*?

The flashing forth of love, bliss, brilliant shards of understanding, exquisite visions of a magical reality—these were coming up for me at lightning speed in the swami's presence, one after another. This was what I'd been looking for. No, it was much more than I had ever imagined was possible. Why would I have said goodbye to the swami? I'd already stepped away from the job that I'd given so much energy to. And as for my marriage . . .

It would have been obvious to any dispassionate observer that Tom and I no longer truly had a marriage, but I was not a dispassionate observer—even with my moment of truth with the swami's translator. People matter in life, enormously, and I *couldn't* just say to Tom that I was leaving him. What I did say was that I wanted to travel with the swami for a while—six months, maybe a year. After that we would see. Tom and I had enough savings that my being away for that length of time wasn't really an issue, especially since I'd be living simply.

I gave two weeks' notice at the *Bulletin*, and in that time I folded my tent and was ready to move on.

9. ᔆᖁ On the Road

I LEFT HAWAII on a red-eye special and arrived in Denver late the next morning with my suitcase and an address. I was excited and more than a little nervous. I didn't have doubts about what I was doing, but it was a big step. When I reached the address, by cab, the swami and most of his party had left, minutes before, and were en route to a weekend retreat site in the mountains above the city. A van with kitchen implements was leaving just then, and there was room in the back for me, my suitcase, and Lynne.

Lynne was a plump woman from Hawaii with the honeyed voice of a Sunday-school teacher and an annoying tendency to see everything that happened as a divine blessing. When I'd met Lynne at the retreat in Honolulu, I had felt a marked disinterest in getting to know her better. I'd tried to disguise that, however, and now I was glad I had. I was such a long way from home, and seeing Lynne's warm smile was like finding family. I hadn't realized until that very moment just how frightened and alone I felt. I'd embarked on this adventure of following an Indian holy man, with almost no preparation or contemplation, and no real idea of what I was stepping into. Through the hour's drive to the mountains, I gratefully chattered with Lynne. And when we found our quarters in one of the decrepit shacks of this down-at-the-heels Boy Scouts camp and saw that we would be sleeping in bunk beds without mattresses, I heard, with new respect, Lynne's chorus of angelic reactions: "Isn't that sweet!"

"It's so rustic!" Perhaps she was right: maybe it was all a divine blessing.

Certainly, the fact that Lynne was there to greet me was of supreme benefit to me. She wasn't staying much longer on tour—she left at the end of that weekend, and I saw her only once again, years later, at the ashram. I remembered then just how valuable this woman turned out to be in my life; how without her presence, a transition that was undeniably difficult might have been impossible. I might not have been strong enough to stay in the swami's world without the smiling welcome of a person whose very warmth, at our first meeting, I'd found annoying. It was a humbling thought, and it supported the swami's declaration that there is divinity in all beings.

The instruction to look for the divine spark in each other, which the swami frequently made in his lectures, is no empty homily. On one level, it's practical advice for survival. How can you possibly guess who will be with you when you need help? And, in that moment, that person *is* God for you, no matter how you may have seen her in less challenging circumstances. There are, of course, many more dimensions to this profound teaching of universal divinity, but when I first joined the swami's staff, my world was pretty much centered on me.

◆ ◆ ◆

WHEN WE GOT to the campgrounds, the swami's translator intercepted me, saying, "The swami was just asking about you. He was asking, 'When is that reporter coming?'"

I didn't stop to consider that it was in any way remarkable that a man who had met hundreds of people in Honolulu, and hundreds more since then, should remember me and recall that I was soon due to arrive. The thought of him had been so paramount in my own mind, the feeling of his presence had been so strong, that I was surprised he didn't already know I was there.

The translator took my arm and led me to the dining

room, where the swami was seated, with just a few people gathered informally around him. The swami smiled and told me he'd just been talking about me, and I, having just heard that, was still not impressed that I was on a saint's mind, and in the very hour of my arrival. The swami told me then that I should eat—I should eat a lot.

That surprised me. I'd been eating very lightly in the two weeks since I'd last been with the swami, even fasting on some days. It was clear that meditation, the power of meditation, was a cleansing force, and of course I should help this cleansing along, right? And what better way to cleanse the physical organs than to eat less!

Eating less had made me even thinner than usual— supermodel slender, from my perspective; an underfed skinny to most. Obviously, that was the way the swami saw it, and I considered that I had his permission to eat more, perhaps even to get fat. Initially, I found the thought relaxing, and I decided that I would eat more.

◆ ◆ ◆

THE NEXT MORNING I rose at three o'clock, another practice I'd been following since I'd last seen the swami. The other side of helping the cleansing along was to meditate as much as I could—several hours a day, morning and evening. On this morning I picked my way through the array of darkened cabins until I found the one that had been designated the meditation hall—actually, it was the dining hall, the bookstore, and the registration area as well. But at this hour, it was clearly meant for meditation.

A swarthy young man was there; he was on the swami's tour staff, the person responsible for transforming the dining area of a Boy Scouts camp into a meditation hall—the carpets were laid, but the lights were up full blast, and there were big framed pictures going up on the walls, and tables being put in place. I didn't offer to help, and instead, I asked if he'd mind my meditating. At his surprised nod, I parked myself in the center of the carpet on the left side (which I knew to be the women's side), facing the swami's chair, assumed a half lotus, and closed my eyes.

As this man put the room together around me, I began doing what I saw as my purificatory work: my entire body shook, and I went into the *bhastrika pranayama*. After about fifteen minutes, the man setting up the room came over and tapped me on the shoulder. I opened my eyes and found him leaning into my face, smiling. He said, "I just want you to know that I feel really good about you doing your thing here and me doing mine."

In that moment I had an inkling that my behavior was eccentric, but I felt utterly accepted, utterly protected. I smiled up at him and withdrew once again into my own undulating, vibrating reality.

After my meditation had become still, I opened my eyes and saw that the hall was dark and almost filled with silent, motionless meditators. The swami was sitting in his chair. Oh. Maybe I shouldn't have sat in the middle of the carpet. Maybe I should have sat at the *front*. If I had, I'd be close to the swami now. I looked around. There was a seat that I could easily slide into, one row closer to the front and one seat closer to the center aisle than where I was. Common sense restrained me: it would be silly to move—I'd be only three feet closer, and the hall was dark besides. I started to close my eyes, to sink back into the sweetness of meditation, when a little voice inside me said, *Move*. But that really didn't make any sense. Again, the voice said, *Move*.

I'd been following inner urgings for the last several weeks, following them with delight, with relief, with gratitude. For years I'd seen other people take inner guidance, something that I myself never seemed to receive. I'd look for signs to tell me what I should do, cues from the universe. I tried to be rational, to watch carefully for cues from other people. And then what I did was often . . . well, off-mark, and sometimes jarringly so. This was frightening, as if severe recompense were going to be demanded because I was so out of sync with the rest of humanity. It was impossible to explain to others that I meant well, that I just didn't know. I felt as if I were a reed with no center, a pretend person, the one human being in whom God had forgotten to implant a soul.

Just two weeks before, back in Honolulu, I'd been driving down Kapiolani Boulevard, one of the main thoroughfares, wondering how to maneuver through all the things that needed to be done before I could join the swami. What should I do first? What should I do in this very moment?

A little voice inside said, *Take off your wedding ring.* I pulled up to a stoplight. I sat for a brief moment without moving. *Take off the ring,* the voice said again. I pulled the gold band—rough gold, wide and heavy—from my left ring finger and felt an opening, a new space in my heart. I had to let go of my life to make room for something else. That's what this was all about. And then I caught my breath in pure wonder: That had come from inside me. I now knew what to do, and it wasn't because someone had told me. This was mine alone.

The voice had led me through a lot in the next two weeks, and so now, as I sat in the meditation hall, when I heard it so clearly, even though what was being asked of me didn't make much sense, it was such a small thing. There was probably some cosmic reason for it, and I didn't really have to understand what that was. I was being told to move . . . so I moved.

The swami started yelling, in Hindi. I didn't understand, but I had a feeling it involved me. It did. A moment later, the translator ran over to me and motioned for me to follow him to the back, where he told me, "The swami has said that you should leave the hall right now. You should not meditate any more this weekend. You can go to your room now and sleep."

Not meditate? There was no question about my trust in this person who had introduced me to all of this, whose love I could feel inside me at times—but not *meditate?* That was the last thing I expected to hear. I went back to my bunk, crawled into my sleeping bag, and slept until breakfast. It wasn't clear to me what was wrong, because the feeling of connection to this inner voice, this inner knowing, was so undeniably valid. It was so obviously a divine force. You could call it God if you wanted to, you could call it *shakti*, the cosmic power, and wasn't that what the swami himself was completely in tune with? "Like a cosmic tuning fork," one of the speakers in the retreat had said in describing him. I loved that image; it was true to my experience—when I was in tune with that inner force, I was in tune with the swami. But here was the swami, disagreeing, angry with me, it seemed, because I was following that very voice he himself had told me to listen to. He had awakened that voice; I had been so sure he *was* that voice.

Well, almost sure. I'd noticed, it was impossible not to notice, that there was more than one voice inside me. At times it seemed I was involved in a dialogue—as I had been that very morning— and at times it seemed as if a mass of warring factions had taken residence inside me. If I'd thought about it objectively, I might have recognized that this had always been the case; this is why I'd stopped listening to my mind in the first place. So I didn't have to hear this cacophony. With my newfound sensitivity, I was tuning in to it as if for the first time. It seemed as if some invisible membrane had been removed, some shell that I'd lived in unawares. Its absence left me vulnerable, open to excruciating tortures but also to ecstasy like I'd never before known.

When I had questions for people around the swami— which I often did—some replies were breezy, some curt; others were clearly impatient, given with a roll of the eye or a slight grimacing of the mouth. It was probably the way I myself had been with Lynne just a few weeks before. Now I knew how my responses might have felt to her. The people I questioned could have been tired or thinking of something else, but to me—for whom every gesture of the universe had meaning, for whom every dust mote that came to my attention was a sign from God—it felt as if the Almighty himself must be displeased with me, and I would be deeply pained until something happened that showed approval: someone smiling at me, for instance, or the appearance of something edible and sweet, or a fly landing on my hand in a warm and companionable way. It didn't take much to move me. Everything was intense.

◆ ◆ ◆

THE TOUR WAS in New York before the swami told me I could meditate again, and it wasn't until we got to Georgia that I understood why he'd had me stop. At this point I was in charge of answering telephones, which meant that I spent most business hours sitting in the office, fielding questions and taking messages. One afternoon a call came in from a man who was clearly distraught. He was a hatha yoga teacher who, following his meeting with the swami, had transmitted his now-enlivened *shakti* to his own students, awakening them. Now, one of these students was in such a state of euphoria that she refused to sleep or eat and tried to put her fist through a plate-glass window because, she explained, she wanted to watch the glass break.

The swami happened to be walking by the office. He had the translator tell this man to have his student eat good, wholesome food and get some sleep, and to have her stop meditating until she came down. As he left the office, the swami told me this was what would have happened to me if I'd kept on meditating.

Awakened spiritual energy, though inherently beneficent, can become too intense for the good of its vehicle—if, as it was with me, the vehicle isn't pure enough to handle all that power or isn't being cared for properly in regard to fuel and rest. If the one who's running the vehicle feels, as I had, that it's fine to ignore common sense. In listening to inner directives from the *shakti*, one must also follow common sense.

But then, common sense might have kept me from following the swami in the first place.

I'm getting ahead of myself. After the Boy Scouts camp, the next stop on the swami's tour was Aspen, which was a relief. Aspen, I knew. Aspen, I had vacationed in. Aspen, the treasure trove of boutiques and gift shops and cozy cafés for coffee and lunch—it was the perfect place to be for those hours in the day when I wasn't with the swami. And there was no retreat in Aspen. This was going to be just like a vacation!

And then it wasn't.

10. ✣ Cleaning Up a Bit

THE SWAMI PROTECTED NEW INITIATES the way a farmer protects a freshly planted field. He wanted to give the newly awakened *kundalini* the support of steady spiritual practice and good company—what's needed to help this power grow—and he wasn't going to let us squander his gift on indulging in a great time in the Rocky Mountains. "Of course, once the tree is mature," he used to say, "you can take down the fence. The tree is tall then, and anyone can come and enjoy its shade."

On Monday, following the morning chant, it was announced there would be a special four-day workshop in Aspen, beginning the following day. "I wonder if I should take the workshop," I said to one of the swami's staff, a fresh-faced teenager who spent her days working in the kitchen.

"It would be a shame not to," she said, "after you came all this way."

That was undeniably true, but I paid the $25 or $30 fee with the vague misgiving that I was being leashed.

Something extraordinary happened in that workshop, during one of the swami's talks. I was only half-listening to him. I was sitting cross-legged on the floor and, at that point, had been there for hours. Sitting had been an issue before, but now I seemed to have developed a new relationship with my hamstring muscles and knees, which, just then, were quiet. I sat erect, feeling like a yogini. I had an image of myself as a little girl, playing King of the Mountain, a game I'd never much liked.

The idea was to take a high spot on the landscape, previously designated as "the mountain," and hold it against all attacks. The preferred method of battle in our neighborhood was a tap of the hand, but the frailties of being nearsighted and shy—of not seeing my antagonists until they were virtually on top of me and of being reluctant to commit so aggressive an act as actually touching them—made me less than adept at this sport. Now, sitting in the meditation hall, I sensed with a thrill the power of the king. I was tall. I was proud. I was invincible.

I could feel energy gathering in the area of my heart. And then, without warning, there was an inner explosion, a *craa-ack* that sounded like a cannon going off in my chest, and, with that, a sudden rush of energy and the sound of the mantra the swami had given me pulsing inside me like a drum. My entire body tingled; the sensation that had begun in my heart radiated out from my body.

The swami stopped speaking. He whipped his head around and looked me straight in the eye. I was in ecstasy. Love was pouring out of me, and there seemed to be no end to it; there was no limit to the love in my heart. The mantra, too, kept on pulsing.

The swami smiled at me. He nodded his head and then turned back to his lecture. And his translator, standing beside the swami, smiled at me as well and nodded his head.

I thought, *This is it. I'm enlightened.*

I had met the swami three weeks before; I'd been practicing meditation regularly for only that time. It was the height of naiveté to think that, in three weeks, I might have completed the spiritual journey that took the swami himself nine years after his awakening, and that following twenty-five years of arduous practice. But I was naive, and arrogant as well.

I thought, *Well. Now what?* I didn't want to go back to Honolulu. After all, I'd just left. New York? Too cold. Someplace warm would be good. Tahiti. I'd always wanted to go to Tahiti: the tropical paradise I'd hoped Hawaii would be. Pictures came before me: coconut palms on a stretch of sand . . . a turquoise sea, diamonds of brilliant sunlight dancing across the face of a cove . . . a shady thatched hut . . . me in a pareu, some authentic native design in warm colors, tied simply around the neck . . . black Ray-Bans . . . and this new power in my heart.

Heart. What had happened to my heart? There was no feeling in my heart. It was gone. The infinite stream of love, the pulsing mantra, the invincibility—all of it gone.

I looked at the swami; he didn't look back. He was into his lecture, on meditation or mantra. If I'd listened to him in that moment, I might have gotten a clue about what had just happened. He led us into meditation then, and with the lights down I was able to indulge the exquisitely painful sense of loss. I'd been offered the pearl beyond price, and I'd thrown it away on a daydream. I cried and cried and cried—embarrassed, bitter, remorseful tears.

I took my lunch to a stream that ran along one side of the schoolyard, and, sitting on some rocks by the water, I contemplated the morning. So it wasn't enlightenment, that much was certain. It was probably the opening of my heart center. The opening and the closing of my heart center. But maybe that wasn't really what had happened: could a spiritual center close again? The swami was always saying that once the goddess Kundalini was awakened, she never went back to sleep. But what had happened? Maybe it could be turned around again really easily.

That afternoon, during the time for questions, I gathered my courage and raised my hand high. The swami was looking down as I started speaking. I heard my voice, as if from a distance, say, "Is it possible that once the heart chakra opens, it can close again . . . ," and then, in another voice, from inside, came a word I hadn't planned to say, came the thing I hadn't wanted to admit: "forever."

With that word, the swami lifted his eyes and looked at me with an expression so loving and compassionate that I almost started crying again, right there, in the middle of that well-lit room and in front of all those people. The swami said that the energy might seem to slacken for a while. He said there are two causes for that. One cause is that if your body is not sufficiently strong to withstand the impact of the *shakti*, then the *shakti* reduces its intensity for a while to strengthen the body. The other is the lack of faith, or disappearance of faith, in the guru—or indifference, insensitivity, or lack of reverence toward him—and that, too, may stop working for a while. But the *shakti*, once it has been awakened, cannot be put to sleep permanently again.

The swami added that there was once a great saint in Karnataka who said that once you have received the guru's touch, the guru's compassion, you can never lose it. Once you've received that energy, it will always work within you.

I wept again in the next meditation, but these were tears of gratitude: I was in the hands of an all-embracing energy, and that energy wasn't going to let go, even if I made a mistake.

◆ ◆ ◆

THAT NIGHT, I curled up in my baby-blue nylon sleeping bag and realized I felt flu-ish. Achy and feverish, just on the verge of nausea; I was really sick. I spent hours trying to get comfortable. I sweat, and fever shot through my body; I threw off the sleeping bag, and two minutes later I shook with chills. I covered up again, and then the burning came back . . . and on and on it went.

I thought I might be dying. I wanted to die. I had a gnawing worry about what would happen to me, sick and depleted, in this unfamiliar world. I was sleeping in someone else's living room. I'd met her only yesterday. I couldn't remember her name, and she probably didn't know mine, either. How would she feel if I died on the floor of her house? Was I contagious?

Sometime in the early morning, I descended into sleep. When I awoke, a couple of hours later, I was wet with perspiration, my sleeping bag drenched, but I was well. The fever had passed, and I felt fine, even refreshed. I laid the sleeping bag out in the sun, took a heavenly shower, and went through the whole day with hardly a thought about my night of travail—until that night, when I crawled back into my sleeping bag and the same thing happened again: the aches, the fire, the sweats, the chills. The only difference was that now I understood: this was purification. This was the working of Kundalini. This was the omniscient inner deity the swami had spoken of, and she was taking me through a yogic cleansing in the only time I had available.

It reminded me of a fairy tale. I felt like the miller's daughter who chose to know her husband only at night, when no one could see them together. Here I was, locked in a private, intimate encounter with a goddess who had designed this whole experience especially for me—and who continued it every night for the rest of our stay in Aspen. Actually, I say "goddess" now, but at the time my understanding was that the energy, the experience, the onset of the fever each evening and its disappearance each morning—all of this—was the work of the swami. I don't think I ever even mentioned this experience to anyone. I saw it as our own little secret: I was laden with inner dreck, and the swami was, in the most private and efficient manner possible, taking it away.

At the dancing *saptah* that was the finale of the next weekend's retreat, back at the Boy Scouts camp, I was gripped by nausea so virulent that I could barely move. I crept outside, hoping the crisp night air would revive me, and found myself kneeling in the bushes, my stomach churning. I heaved several times, and at first it seemed that nothing was coming up. Then I realized that something was being expelled from me, something subtle but nonetheless palpable: a noxious black mass, which I could certainly feel and almost see. And with each forceful expulsion of air, my midsection felt lighter, cleaner. I felt that the swami was with me, his hand on my shoulder. Someone I had never seen before helped me to my feet, handed me a drink of water. As I held this person's arm and walked back into the hall, getting stronger with each step, I felt the swami supporting me. A surrogate was beside me, a ministering angel who had suddenly appeared with a glass of cool water, but the real author of that gesture was the one who had awakened the inner energy in the first place, the one who had warned me what would happen with it and explained why it would happen, the one who was now watching my every move with a fatherly concern to make sure I was given the right support. Clearly, in my mind, it was all the swami. Now I might say that the swami was one with the power, the Power, that is author of all.

When I got back into the hall, I chanted and danced for the rest of the night. In those days, it wouldn't have occurred to me to pace myself, to save something for tomorrow. It wasn't time yet for me to learn that.

11. ᴄʀ *In the Family*

I SAT WITH MY MOM just inside the front door of a large living room, much like the other large living rooms I had seen on the swami's tour. Most of the furniture and all of the artwork had been removed. There was one large, overstuffed chair at the far end of the room; this was where the swami sat, speaking quietly in melodious Hindi to the tour manager, to his secretary, to others on staff with a question about what should happen at this particular tour stop: Oklahoma City. It was midmorning, the time when the swami conducted business, and anyone who wished to could join him. There were perhaps two dozen people in the room—some waiting their turn, some sitting with their eyes closed—and then there was my mother, who glared at the swami as if she might kill him, this ogre who had ruined her daughter's perfect life.

Before leaving Hawaii, I'd called my parents to give them the news that I was going to be traveling with an Indian holy man I'd interviewed. They were Episcopalians, Republicans who subscribed to *Reader's Digest* and played gin rummy with their friends. The idea of meditation was foreign to them. My parents had their own daily practice, involving gin (my mother's path) and scotch (my father's). They were *not* alcoholics, my mother used to tell me when I was growing up and, with more perspicacity than tact, used to star, underline, and otherwise flag for them pertinent magazine articles on social alcoholism. "You've never missed a meal because of my drinking," she said. "Your father's never missed a day of work." And that was true; my parents functioned well within the parameters of their world. Oh, they fought, almost constantly, but, as my mother explained, "everyone fights." Then at college I'd had a revelation: people living together did not have to yell at each other.

When I graduated, I moved to Hawaii, as far from my parents geographically as I could manage. They were perplexed. "People *visit* Hawaii," my mother said; "they don't *live* there." Then I married a man as different from the men in my family as I could manage: a man who preferred reading to watching televised sports; a man who played tennis, rather than riding around on a golf cart; a man who never liked to raise his voice. This choice also surprised my parents. No one put it into words, not to my face, but they were shocked that I was marrying—a *Jew!* My father had never spoken the word in my presence; my mother used *jew* as a verb. Tom was eminently presentable, however. He was agreeable, witty, attractive, successful; we were both successful professionally, and for my parents that was what mattered most. They became quite satisfied with the direction my life had taken. They visited us in Hawaii and found that people do, indeed, live there.

Then I dropped this latest piece of news about my life plans, the swami, and my parents were once again speechless. My paternal grandmother summed up the family's reaction with the only positive spin she could put on it: "Over the years, Peggy, you have provided us with many interesting topics for conversation."

I'd thought that was the end of it, and when I realized that the swami would travel from Colorado to Oklahoma City, just a hundred miles from my parents' home in Tulsa, I was thrilled. Surely, if they met the swami, they, too, would feel the force of his beneficent power.

That wasn't quite the way it happened. My father was away on a business trip, and Mom, the more irascible of the two, was looking anything but mollified by the experience of sitting in the swami's presence. I thought that if I could maneuver her into a direct verbal exchange with him, she would feel better about everything—the swami, my being here, her being here. A couple of times, I leaned over and whispered, "Mom, I'd like to introduce you to the swami. . . ."

The first time, she whispered back, "I don't want to meet him. I just want to watch." She didn't move her eyes from him as she spoke; she seemed to be involved in some sort of internal diatribe, the specifics of which I really didn't want to know.

The second time I asked her, she said, "Peggy, I will *not* meet him."

By then I had begun to understand how clearly the swami saw any group of people. He couldn't have missed the two of us sitting there: me and this well-dressed, middle-aged woman who was glaring at him, hissing to me that she wouldn't meet him.

◆ ◆ ◆

I LET THE drama with my mother slip away. A young woman brought a baby for the swami to bless. The new mother had a sturdy build, light brown hair, and a smile so radiant that it made her and everything she did beautiful. She was like a queen, holding up her infant son to the swami with the grace of one presenting a treasure. The baby, pink-cheeked and round, was laughing, and the swami laughed right back, the two of them locked eye to eye in an exchange only they could fathom.

This idyllic, ordinary scene had never been enacted in my own life. Sinking into the bliss of it, I had to wonder, why had my face never been so suffused with love? Why had I never been a mother? For years I'd taken for granted that at some point I would have children. What had happened to that certainty? The poignancy of this question triggered an ache in my belly. The desire to expand and bear fruit was tangible. Scenes came into my mind: my mother screaming at me her litany of years past: "Just *wait* till you have children of your own," and I, with the silent defiance of a child who dared not talk back, thinking, *Never. I am never having children.*

Now, of course, I never would have children. I had just left my husband. My life was going in another direction entirely. Tom and I had thought about children. I'd asked him about it once. I looked at the wives of other lawyers in his firm, all of them mothers, and saw that while I worked ten, twelve hours a day, six days a week, putting out a section of a daily newspaper, they took their children to the beach, they went shopping, they learned to make ceramics at the local art institute. I'd always wanted to make ceramics. One evening, I turned to my husband and said, very brightly, "Let's have a child." He thought that was a fine idea and said that the paper would surely give me a six-month maternity leave. But that wasn't what I'd had in mind, six months off, and I said, "I think it might be nice just to be a mother." He said he was afraid I'd be bored. I thought, *He's afraid I'll be boring.*

What I was seeing before me wasn't boring. It was heaven. It was love in action. There was an unutterable beauty in this woman's most minute gestures, the way she brushed back her son's curls and moved his tiny arm from his own belly so she could press his whole body against her breast—against her heart. My own heart was melting as I watched her. In the center of my chest, I could feel the love radiating between this mother and child. Tears slipped down my cheeks, and I brushed them away with my fingertips, not wanting my mother to see me so emotional.

We were a mother and child watching a mother and child, and I gave my mother a sidelong look to see how this poignant scene was striking her. She was still glaring at the swami, her face even fiercer than the last time I'd looked. I marveled at how we were sitting side by side, almost on top of each other, in that crowded little room, yet we were in totally different realities. I was in heaven, or at least in purgatory—going over an aspect of my life I'd never looked at closely, preparing to let go of an attachment I hadn't even been aware I had. My mother, only inches away, was exploring an inner hell, raging silently at the fiend who she felt had destroyed her daughter's life.

This scene reminds me of something the swami's successor once said about the swami. She used to see him in the morning putting little things into his pocket—bracelets, pieces of wrapped candy, and small toys—and then, at the end of the day, she would watch him take out these objects and line them up on his bureau. The next day, it would be the same: in the morning he stuffed his pockets with small items, and in the evening he brought them back again. She wondered why the swami did this, and then one day he told her those were little gifts he took with him to give to people, and each day he brought them back because, as he said, "Nobody wants anything."

And so it was here. The swami had laid out this lovely tableau of a mother offering her child to God, yet how many people wanted this gift? How many accepted it? My own mother wasn't even aware of it.

I, on the other hand, received a sense of closure. Having children hadn't been such a divine experience for my mother, and it isn't for many women. If I had been a mother, I would not have been traveling with the swami. I would have been trapped in Honolulu, caring for that tiny being whose survival depended on me.

◆ ◆ ◆

WHEN MY FATHER returned from his business trip, he and my mother came together to see the swami. Mom had packed a picnic lunch for the three of us, and, at my strongly worded invitation, they arrived early enough to join that morning's "semiprivate" *darshan*—the swami's meeting with a small group gathered for the express purpose of talking with him. This time there would be no sitting silent at the back of the room.

Before we went in, Mom said, "I don't have the slightest idea what to say to him."

"It doesn't have to be anything special," I told her. "Just whatever comes up for you." She took me at my word.

The swami was giving a meditation retreat at the time, and this *darshan* took place at the retreat site in a barnlike room with high ceilings, like a high school gymnasium. Thirty or forty people were clustered in this commodious space, and the sparseness of the group was unsettling, as if the organization were wearing buildings too large for its modest needs. A huge chair was at the center of a wall, and we all sat facing it, some on the floor, my parents and I on metal folding chairs in the back. Seeing this makeshift meditation hall through their eyes, I knew it didn't look good. It didn't look established or safe or in any way familiar. Why was that sheaf of feathers propped up against the swami's chair? And the large photograph of a big-bellied, naked man—what was that about? My father was a big man (six foot four, 220 pounds), and he shifted his posterior from one cheek to the other every few minutes; the chair wasn't large enough to accommodate all of him at once. Dad kept eyeing the swami's chair, the only comfortable seat in the room.

After the swami strode in, people were called forward one group at a time. When our turn came, we walked up to the swami: I on the left, Mom in the center, and Dad, ramrod straight, on the right. I dropped to my knees and brushed my forehead against the floor, as I was accustomed to doing—then, inexplicably, I remained on my knees through the entire conversation. My mother accomplished a little genuflection of the sort Episcopalians do just before communion. Dad didn't budge. Taking my mother's hand, I told the swami that these were my parents, George and Grace Dunsmoor, and they had wanted to meet him. This was my offering to the moment, and really all I could manage just then.

The swami smiled graciously and asked my father how he "found" me now.

I was obviously happy, healthy, stronger than I had ever been, so there was a lot my father could have noticed, could have said in this moment. His reply was brief as a gunshot: "Fine." It was all my father said in the entire conversation, and this one word was expelled with a force and fury so intense that I blinked as I heard it. I wanted to keep my eyes shut, but I didn't dare.

Mom stepped in, speaking in her gracious-lady voice, the

verbal expression of a person determined to say what ought to be said. "Peggy looks good," she said. "She's gained weight." People in the room laughed, and I realized that after a lifetime of prompting me to eat more, my mother had found an unexpected ally in the swami. "She seems happy," Mom went on, "and we're glad to see that.

"We were surprised when she said she was going to leave her husband." My mother began to warm now, getting to the heart of what she wanted to say. "Whatever Peggy wants to do is fine with us, you know, but it all happened so quickly. One minute she was in Hawaii, and the next she'd left. She left her job. She left her husband. I know that what you're doing here must be good, but I didn't think that she would leave her husband—"

The swami cut in: "He was a lawyer, wasn't he?"

I pressed my lips together, swallowing a giggle that was trying to come up. God, did he have my mother's number! I shot her a quick, sidelong look to catch her reaction. She had heard the words but not the spin that launched them.

"Yes, and a very fine lawyer," she said. "He is a nice man. We were happy when she married him and very surprised when she said she was going to leave him. . . ."

As my mother continued, her face took on a glow. She was giving voice to her thoughts, her real reservations about what I had done, and expressing herself bountifully, offering herself to the swami earnestly and wholeheartedly—and so he could give to her in return. On his way out of the room later, he stopped and spoke again to my mother and, smiling, gave her a small vial of *hina*, a precious scented oil. She, too, was smiling, charmed by him, for that moment utterly in love with him. By the time we got to our picnic lunch, she was a little more reserved.

Throughout most of her life, she got a lilt in her voice whenever she spoke about the swami. Eventually she gave me the *hina*, and I saved it for her. When she died, I bathed her body in it, grateful for this earthy fragrance and the blessings it contained.

12. ❧ My Gargoyle

I CALLED TOM from the Los Angeles airport and was surprised at how happy I was to hear his voice. I was on my way back to Hawaii to help prepare for the swami's next visit and, the plan was, to divorce Tom.

"Where will you be staying?" he asked.

I wasn't sure. I was flying in with others on the advance crew, and while I knew some housing arrangement must have been made, I had no idea what it might be.

"You *could* stay here," Tom said. "You know . . . sleep on the couch."

I left it open. I was tempted. The invitation was warm, the prospect of "going home" comforting, and the idea of being with Tom again raised echoes of a long-held personal dream. I had *so* wanted our marriage to work.

We'd met on an interview. I'd been in Hawaii about a year and was researching an article on teen drug use—then a new topic. Tom, who had just moved to the islands from New York, was the local authority on an obscure legal case I needed to understand. He was intelligent, good-looking, tall, and a bit shy, which I liked because I, too, was tall and shy. Our interview was unremarkable, but he called a few days later and we started going out—every night. One evening we got stoned, and when he put his arms around me, I felt there was no separation, no physical boundary, between us. I couldn't tell where my skin stopped and his began. And we were fully clothed.

A few nights later, I stood on the edge of a suitcase to see what my dress looked like in the medicine-cabinet mirror—not the most brilliant of my ideas—and I fell, breaking my arm. Tom suggested I move in with him so I had someone to help me with buttons and zippers, and I just never moved out. A few months later he said, "Why don't we get married?" It seemed like a good idea. We called it love, and, more to the point, we fit each other's pictures: I saw in him my Harvard-educated lawyer, and he saw me as his long-legged shiksa.

Tom and I were married in Tulsa, at my parents' home. In their life together Mom and Dad built four houses, starting small and gaining a bit in size and tone as they went. These were all three bedrooms–two baths, set in neighborhoods where, though the dwellings are not all alike, they are obviously created by people with the same vision. The Tulsa house was my parents' second, the one where I had grown up. It was not a tract home but almost, and I could tell from their expressions that Tom's sister and brother-in-law were not favorably impressed. His mother wasn't either, but there's really nothing she would have liked. She looked at the wedding cake and said, "What? No food?" For the most part, everyone tried to be friendly, tried to ignore the fact that they had nothing in common.

Officiating was a judge, a common pleas judge, because that was all my mother could get for our union, which was, in Tulsa in 1968, considered a "mixed marriage." "People like you have a right to get married," the judge had told Tom and me the day before, "but I'm elected. Please don't tell anyone I did this."

We honeymooned in New York City. It was my first time there, so I gaped at the buildings. We stayed the first night at the Plaza, with chocolate mints on our pillows, and after that in an East Side apartment with chocolate-colored walls. The apartment belonged to a friend of Tom's who was going away on vacation. He told us chocolate walls were the latest thing; people felt the color set off paintings to good advantage. Another of Tom's friends showed us her own paintings: lines of color in waves across white canvas. Her work, all variations on the same theme, was in galleries and was gaining recognition. "I don't know what it is I'm doing," she said. "I just feel like doing it." I didn't know what she was doing, either. I didn't know what to say about any of this—the brown walls, the wavy paintings—and I felt like such a rube.

Hair opened on Broadway that season. Tom and I got stoned one evening and went to see it. Walking down the steps to the New York subway with the kind of heightened awareness that comes with psychedelics, I became acutely aware of my fear. I was walking in an alien world and felt I could at any moment make a misstep and fall. As I looked down the subway steps, it seemed a long drop to the bottom.

Our first weekend back in Hawaii, I dived into the Pacific Ocean at Queen's Surf, the beach young professionals then preferred, and lost my wedding ring. I could feel it come off. I was frantic. I started shrieking, and within a few minutes some two dozen people—Tom among them—were combing the sand in the shallow water, trying to help find my ring.

At one point I stopped, looked straight up into the bright blue tropical sky, and said, "I. Want. That. Ring." There was outrage in my voice. I couldn't have told you to whom or to what I was speaking, but my intent was steely and the answer was immediate. My right hand, seemingly of its own volition, plunged into two feet of water and three inches of sand—and came up with the ring.

It was a stunning experience. Though I didn't truly think it through, there was one aspect of this event I couldn't avoid seeing, even in that moment. When my wedding ring, the most visible symbol of my marriage, fell away, I demanded of the universe that it be returned to me. I was approaching this marriage as an act of personal will, and I knew I had better give it my best shot.

I did just that. It was an unspoken reality of our marriage that I cared more about it than Tom did, tried harder to make it succeed, and also put up more barriers to keep that from happening. My anger was closer to the surface than his, my ego larger and more easily bruised, my ability to articulate and defend a point of view less developed, my sense of self more damaged. Emotionally speaking, I was about four; Tom may have been twelve.

◆ ◆ ◆

IN OUR FIRST year together, we went on a weekend trip to Kauai with two other couples. Actually, we'd planned to go with one of the couples, and then the wife from the second couple, Betsy, asked if they could be included. We said yes, but I was reluctant. I had trouble with Betsy, found her overbearing, and had been looking forward to an outing without her. On this trip Betsy said something that triggered me—it was insignificant; something about the coffee—and I let a fire stream of rage erupt that shocked us all. It certainly shocked me. It was exactly the kind of thing my mother had always done, the kind of thing I hated.

As it turned out, the event was a trigger to positive change, and the woman I'd had so much trouble with turned out to be a friend after all. Betsy was studying psychology, undergoing therapy with a psychologist I'd recommended to her—someone I'd interviewed and then seen a few times myself before I'd met Tom. She told this psychologist about my flare-up. He pointed out to her that I hadn't gotten angry with anyone else; I was at fault, certainly, but it must have had something to do with her. When Betsy told him who I was and that I'd been in therapy with him myself, he said, "Oh, yes. I was sorry when she stopped coming. I didn't feel we had finished."

Betsy called me with this message and her own contemplation about her role in the weekend. We both apologized, and I admitted to myself that I needed to do something—as I put it at the time—to clean up my act. Making an appointment with this therapist seemed like the right first step.

When I told Tom what I wanted to do, he said women who saw therapists were like women who got manicures and did lunch and kept toy poodles; this was not something he wanted for his wife. We were arguing a lot at that time. From Tom's perspective, the arguments were my fault—and he was probably right—but this one, I knew, was worth having. I needed help to stop myself from sabotaging this marriage that mattered so much to me.

I began seeing the psychologist, and when Tom came along for one session, he was impressed and decided to have his own appointments. The two of them became lifelong friends. This psychologist was a singular individual; he advised businesses and schools, but he also had built his own sailboat and wrote children's books for the fun of it. He was a bit like a village shaman, and Tom and I both benefited from looking at our lives, week by week, through the lens of his wisdom.

We would come home from work or from an evening with friends and talk over in detail what we'd seen and heard. We often shared the same perspective, but Tom added another dimension to those conversations. I loved his dry wit, his gift of mimicry, his clarity. When I was curled up on our couch, talking to Tom, all was right in my world. It was the happiest I'd ever been.

After about four years, our psychologist decided to stop seeing clients. We were far enough along, he said; we didn't need him. And he wanted to do other things now: travel around Europe, do more writing.

Tom and I were both stunned, and, predictably, our responses were quite different. I turned to other modalities, other therapies, with a vengeance, while Tom settled firmly into the practice of business law.

But that was then. If I had changed over the last six months, surely Tom had as well. What if we *could* get back together again? There wasn't animosity between us. We had separated, yes, but we hadn't purposely wounded each other in the process. Perhaps it would be possible for us to pick up our marriage—not where we'd left off, but in some new and wonderful place.

I spent the entire four-hour flight to Honolulu in a gauzy cocoon of remembrance, reliving lovely moments Tom and I had shared. Like the time I got home from interviewing a person with Hansen's Disease—once called leprosy—and, even though the point of my article had been to show how this disease was not contagious, had admitted to Tom that I was terrified I'd caught it. He took hold of my hands and held them. "If you have it," he said, "then so do I."

This extended reverie was unutterably sweet, but the moment I saw Tom at the luggage claim, I knew it was fantasy. The marriage was finished. I don't know how I knew this or why, but the *what* of it was absolutely apparent, as if Tom had been wearing a neon sign on his forehead in huge, glowing letters: NOT HAPPENING.

We hugged, we exchanged awkward small talk, we made plans to meet about the divorce, and when my luggage arrived, I went off with the rest of the advance crew. Tom and I didn't even acknowledge that I might have gone back with him to stay at our house, soon to be his house. It was obviously not the thing to do.

◆ ◆ ◆

OURS WAS A remarkably friendly divorce. Late one afternoon, we sat down in the house and, in half an hour, verbally divvied up our property. Afterward, we went out to dinner. Tom represented us both. I trusted him completely on this, and he was so ethical that after he drew up the papers, he asked a mutual friend, also a lawyer, to look them over to make sure he hadn't shorted me in any way. Neither of us had to go to court, and I never had to meet with anyone other than Tom. The divorce was granted in the judge's chambers. If a divorce can be blessed, ours was.

There was one possession of mine I didn't know what to do with. It was a plaster replica, maybe a foot and a half tall, of a gargoyle, one of the horned, winged creatures that used to guard medieval cathedrals to ward off evil spirits. A college boyfriend had given it to me, and I'd carted it around ever since. Seeing it again, I understood my attachment to the little monster: this was the way I saw myself. It wasn't that I had horns or wings, of course, but on an interior view, I didn't trust myself. I would become angry; I could be mean or self-serving, and, though later I would regret what I'd said or done, it had happened often enough that I knew the pattern—and didn't like it. I suppose you could say I'd never liked myself very much. Or at all.

Now, after several months of living with a saint, I knew the gargoyle didn't fit—it wasn't me anymore; it didn't have to be mine. But what could I do with this symbol of ill omen? Giving it to a friend would be like visiting someone with a curse. And throwing it away didn't seem right, either.

I took the gargoyle with me one day when I went to help clean the house where the swami would be staying. Sitting out on the seawall behind the house, I explained my dilemma to Rick, the yoga teacher. He said, "Throw it in the ocean." To me, that was worse than putting it out with the trash: I would be treating the ocean like a wastebasket!

"I'll give it to the swami," I said. I found a cabinet in the living room that no one would have any reason to open and hid the gargoyle in a back corner—a spot so obscure that I forgot about it.

◆ ◆ ◆

ONE THING I wanted to accomplish on this visit was to introduce Tom to the swami. As I endeavored to set up this *darshan*, I learned that they'd spoken already. At the Maui retreat, right after Tom told me, "This isn't my path," he had stalked down the drive, where he encountered the swami. The swami smiled at him and said something friendly to the effect of, "Can't you stay for the rest of the retreat?" Tom must have folded all of his fear and frustration into one terse "I don't have time," as he continued on down the drive. Six months later, when I told the translator that I wanted to introduce my ex-husband to the swami, he said, "The swami has met him already. I'm sure the swami will remember the meeting. I don't think I'll ever forget it."

Nonetheless, the *darshan* I sought for Tom was arranged. There were about forty people in that morning's gathering. When our turn came, the swami asked Tom if he was going to take the weekend retreat, and Tom said no. The swami then asked if he had gone to any of the programs; Tom reiterated, "No."

I realized I had better step in fast with my purpose. "Swamiji," I said, "please bless him."

The swami looked over at me and made the sound that I always thought of as arising straight from his heart, a kind of *ahhhhhh*, but deep and resonant. "You have a good heart," he told me. He smiled and nodded, and I knew it would be done.

Then Tom said, "I'm sorry the marriage didn't work out."

The swami said, "That happens sometimes." It was a short answer, but a few minutes later two people came up to have their marriage blessed, and to them the swami said what he could not say to Tom: Marriage is not standing side by side, looking at each other. In a marriage you stand together, facing God. You are side by side, looking in the same direction. Otherwise it's not a marriage.

This enlightened view of the main focus of seven years of my life took my breath away. The swami's words put everything into a new and higher perspective. It was the first inkling I'd had that the breakdown in my marriage had nothing to do with personalities. What if it was simply a question of our individual relationships with God? When Tom was an atheist and I an agnostic, there were problems between us, certainly, but we were a couple. We *were* looking in the same direction—or at least we were looking in various directions simultaneously and for similar reasons. But once I was introduced to the realm of spirit, once my questions about the existence of a higher reality had started being answered affirmatively, Tom's deeply rooted faith in materiality was affronted. And from my perspective, exploring this new world was the most exciting option my life had ever offered me.

On the swami's lanai in Honolulu, 1975

♦ ♦ ♦

THE SWAMI WAS going to Maui for a week, and it was decided that I would be part of the staff staying behind on Oahu to make more contacts and invite more people to *satsangs* after his return. I understood that this was because we hadn't done quite enough before his arrival, and, though there was truth in this, I regretted not being able to accompany him to Maui on this trip. Being there with the swami had been extraordinary.

The day before his departure, I was at the swami's house. A small group had gathered informally on the lanai after lunch. At one point, the swami asked if I'd ever been to Maui.

I said, "Yes, Swamiji, the last time I was there was with you." There was definitely a little flavor of something in my answer. Didn't he remember? That was when I'd asked him if I could join his tour. A lot had happened for me on Maui, and the swami had been instrumental in it—or at least he seemed to have been. How much of what went on was he actually able to take in? It was hard to know for sure.

The swami went inside then, and I thought that was all for the afternoon. But a moment later he reappeared, striding out of the house and holding aloft . . . my gargoyle! He said, "The reason I didn't remember you were on Maui is that this is what you looked like then."

I started laughing. I said, "I didn't know what to do with it"—meaning the gargoyle.

He said, "You could throw it in the ocean . . ." He paused for a moment, before he added, "Or you could give it to someone else who sees herself this way. Maybe she'll change like you did."

How could the swami reach into a corner of a closed cupboard to come up with the perfect reply to my thoughts in this very moment? And how could he echo a conversation I'd had three weeks earlier, at a time when he was thousands of miles away? What order of being was this? What were the subtle forces that served him, and how did he beckon them to his will? And this is the simple part of the mystery. The rest happened over time.

I knew immediately who would receive the gargoyle: Nancy, a woman who worked in the *Star Bulletin*'s advertising department. I had met her a year before. She had wry humor and an unassuming air that I liked. In my final months at the paper, we'd had lunch together regularly, trying to turn our various frustrations into laugh lines. While the swami was on Maui, Nancy was one of the people I called. As I gave her the gargoyle, I told her the story behind it and invited her to meet the swami. She came to one of the evening programs the next week, and when I introduced her, I told the swami, "This is the person who now has the gargoyle." He laughed and hit her again and again on the head with a sheaf of peacock feathers.

Years later, I saw Nancy. She still had the gargoyle and knew she'd been blessed.

I was blessed as well, but what came up for me didn't always seem to be beneficent. In the purifying fire of spiritual practice, I began releasing inner demons.

13. ⚭ The Kitchen Wala

BY THE TIME I MET IVAN, I'd already fallen for at least three men on the swami's tour staff. This was a problem because, at this point, the swami's path was a celibate one. He was touring in the West to teach meditation, to introduce the cleansing practices of singing God's name and offering selfless service. Romance was, most emphatically, not the focus of his work as a teacher. A swami is, after all, a monk. Once, when asked about the Indian tradition of seating men and women on opposite sides of the meditation hall, the swami said it was because we are all so beautiful. If we looked at one another, we wouldn't look inside—and this was what we were there to do: look inside ourselves. Another time he said romantic relationships were like a wall that isn't strong enough to hold our weight. He asked if we, hearing this, would listen to him. Or would we climb that wall and find out for ourselves?

I often tried the wall in my first years with the swami, even after I found that, for me, it was a supremely bad choice. I tended toward infatuation. Given even a shard of interest, I would do a lot of mental enhancement. I would fantasize.

Ivan was tall and slender and dark, with curly hair and burning, soulful eyes—a perfect Mephistopheles. I could picture him in a cape. He first approached me at one of the dancing *saptahs* the swami started holding on Saturday evenings in the temporary ashram he'd set up in New York City. The all-night dancing *saptah* had been the Saturday-night feature of meditation

On the swami's US tour, 1975

retreats. Now we had a two-hour dancing *saptah* that was a quick energizer for busy New Yorkers. After the women finished dancing the first round, Ivan approached me, said something innocuous and introductory, and asked if I would like to go for a coffee sometime.

"I don't do that kind of thing," I told him.

He laughed. "What kind of thing is that? You don't drink coffee? I don't care about that. If you like, we could have lemonade . . . Orange juice? . . . Herbal tea?"

He was easy, light. I was unspeakably earnest. I think he found it endearing.

We met on a Saturday evening, we did go for a coffee, and the following Friday I rode with him to a retreat in upstate New York. I enjoyed that ride and, it seems, didn't want it to end, because I got us lost. We arrived after dinner, during an orientation the translator was giving. We sat at the back. The translator was saying that the guru-disciple relationship is sacred, the one significant relationship we have in our lives. Other friends come and go, but this one friend is our true well-wisher; this one friend matters. Then, looking directly at me, the translator said, "I would never think of leaving the ashram without telling the swami where I was going, and with whom."

I have always been suggestible. Even my eyes change color, ranging from moss green to rust and sometimes to amber yellow, depending on the light, my mood, and the colors I happen to have around me. At this perceived rebuke from the translator, which entered my mind like a spark of fire, I felt my ambivalence about romantic involvement coalesce into a burning sense of guilt that kept me awake through much of the night.

The next morning when the swami gave *darshan*, I went forward with resolution to lay my sins at his feet and to become, once again, a disciple. But how would I do this? I couldn't very well apologize for what had happened—what *had* happened? All I'd done was accept a ride from someone without telling the swami! Okay, so I would ask him about everything in the future, starting now.

I dropped my head at the swami's feet, and when I lifted it, I pulled close and said, "I rode up to the retreat yesterday with Ivan. He has asked if I would drive back to the city with him again on Monday. Is that all right with the swami?"

There was a small ripple through the crowd of disciples who were gathered, as always, closely around the swami. What I mean by that is several people turned and looked at me simultaneously. I didn't notice whether Ivan, who was also there, hearing this, was one of them. The swami gave me a brilliant and enigmatic reply. "This is Saturday," he said. "That's Monday. A lot can happen between now and then."

Late that afternoon, the translator found me in the dining hall. He said, "Swamiji wants you to do *seva* in the kitchen, starting tomorrow morning. You can report to the kitchen at 4:00 a.m."

I felt like I'd been thrust into a cold shower. I said, "Do you think this has anything to do with my question this morning?"

"It's apparent to me what it means," the translator said with a frosty smile, "but you'll have to discover that for yourself."

I told Ivan that evening, and later, eleven-ish, he pounded on the translator's door, rousting him from bed to hear, "I never *touched* her!" It seems that Ivan—whose wife had been living at Findhorn, in Scotland, for the last four years, whose rakish charm made him irresistible to many—had a reputation as a womanizer. My public avowal of our connection must have looked like an admission of major proportions.

At four the next morning, I was in the kitchen, chopping onions. The swami came in five minutes later and made coffee for the kitchen *walas* (workers). Milky and sweet, laced with cardamom and nutmeg, it was nectarean. "He's never done this before," someone said after the swami had left, and then I figured it was at least in part for me, to give me something sweet to take in along with my first taste of the guru's discipline.

◆ ◆ ◆

THAT MORNING I found chopping vegetables to be an object lesson in focus. When my attention wavered for even a moment while I was wielding the kitchen's serious, squarish blades, my fingers were likely to taste the steel. I couldn't think about Ivan. I had to think about broccoli, onions, lettuce, beets—and not all at once, either, but one at a time, as they came before me.

My role was scullery maid: fetching, chopping, storing, mopping, never stopping, always hopping. After a few initiations by knife, I was dripping Band-Aids from my left hand. Marty, a rangy nineteen-year-old from Brooklyn, loped around the kitchen like a cherub on stilts and turned an onion into confetti in about thirty seconds flat. Here I was, a woman who had kept house and given dinner parties, who had cooked *boeuf bourguignonne* and moussaka, almost mouthing the steps so I would remember to get my thumb out from under the knife. It was humbling. It was also medicinal.

Over the next two days, each time I saw Ivan, it was a fresh experience. My mind had been otherwise occupied. I hadn't conjured up some idea of what should happen with him, and so whatever did happen was fine. On Monday, though nothing had been said, I knew from inside that it was all right for me to ride back to the city with him. It was apparent to me by then that the swami had put me into the kitchen to protect me not from Ivan but from my own mind, which could have embroidered this tiny romantic adventure with enough fantasy to build it into a major trap.

After we returned to Manhattan, I continued doing *seva* in the kitchen. I found the experience penetrating. By the end of the week, I couldn't remember what it was like *not* to be in the kitchen—not to arise at three thirty from my bed in the second women's dorm, to bathe in the shower that I shared with forty-five other women, to pull clothes out of the suitcase stored at the head of my foam-rubber mattress, and to descend two floors to the kitchen. My three weeks as a kitchen *wala* were, in their intensity, scope, and impact, like a full incarnation.

This universe was utterly real, and then, like the ocean spray that lifts from the top of a wave and flies with the wind, disappearing in midair—angel hair, a friend used to call it—the same universe was suddenly gone. It was gone for me. I was no longer in it.

◆ ◆ ◆

THERE IS A story I heard the swami tell a number of times that captures this quality of existence, the way one reality replaces another in our experience.

In the beginning, Gadhi is living in the house of his guru, following a daily regime of chanting, meditation, and selfless service. One day while meditating, he hears an inner voice: *You are being granted a boon. Whatever you wish will be yours. Just name it.*

Gadhi asks to understand the nature of the world. Actually, he calls it *maya*, in Sanskrit, but in the simplest sense that's what *maya* is: the illusory power that creates the world of form.

The boon bestower tries to convince Gadhi to change his

request. Why would he want to understand the world? He could ask for liberation. Or joy.

Gadhi persists. It is, after all, *his* boon. The next morning, he splashes his face with water—and opens his eyes in another world.

He finds himself in a desolate land. For weeks he wanders, searching in vain for food. To survive, he marries a tribal woman, has children with her, and after years experiencing the minute-by-minute difficulty of scratching out a bare existence, he overhears his own children planning to kill him. At this, he runs away.

Gadhi runs and runs, until finally he reaches a city. He arrives on the day of a big event. Everyone is in the streets, walking to the city's main square. Gadhi finds himself standing in the center of this square with all of the local men. The king has just died with no heir, and, by local tradition, a new king is to be chosen by the royal elephant, a huge, caparisoned beast carrying a garland on his trunk. And whom do you think the elephant garlands? Why, Gadhi, of course. Now our hero becomes a king, leading a life of splendor, making laws, passing judgment when it's called for.

◆ ◆ ◆

IT FELT LIKE that for me. I would spend long mornings in the kitchen, attend the noon chant, and serve lunch, and then after lunch Ivan and I would go out for a few hours. One day we went to the Metropolitan Museum of Art, where he showed me a thousand-year-old statue of the Buddha, one of the original Lohans from China. As I stood before this miraculous, larger-than-life ceramic statue, it became alive for me. It was throbbing with energy, radiating an unearthly light. Another time we went to Ivan's apartment, where he had me taste a pudding he had made for the swami using agar-agar—the perfect thing, he felt, for the guru to eat because, unlike traditional Indian sweets, it was light.

Often while I was out, I would pick up things for other

people in the kitchen. The head cook liked jelly beans ("No green ones, please"), and once I bought her some lipstick. One day I asked her why she never went out herself, and, with the air of someone who has been waiting to speak, she told me, "The swami doesn't like it when people who work in the kitchen leave the ashram."

"Oh really."

"Yes," she said. "The kitchen is a special place. It's like a temple. There's a lot of *shakti* here, and when we take that *shakti* outside, we dissipate it. When we live with it, then the *shakti* can cleanse us, it can purify us. This is the way the swami can give us what he wants us to have."

I let this piece of information sit in my mind for the rest of the day, like a seed gestating. That night, after the final chant, I went back into the kitchen, into this temple, and without putting on the light, I stood by the chopping table, by the scene of so many difficult moments. At times I'd felt badgered, picked on, like I wasn't bright enough or fast enough or good enough to be there. The head cook was quite charismatic, and her words had power. Dramas eddied about her like riptides; it was hard not to get caught in the undertow of this wind-driven water. Escaping the ashram each day had been a matter of survival for me. But what was it the swami wanted me to do?

Did I even have to ask! I wasn't in New York to visit museums. I hadn't come for a romance. I had come to achieve something lasting, something for myself. And that's what the swami wanted for me. I ran the flat of my hand over the surface of the chopping table, the wood nicked and scarred with its service. No romance there, but it was strong, it was useful. Softly, I said aloud, "All right, Swamiji. I promise I won't leave the ashram. I'll stay right here in your temple and drink in your *shakti*."

There was a fly in the kitchen, making wide arcs around me in the moonlight. The moment I spoke, the fly began to buzz my cheek, landing there again and again and again, and with each touch of this tiny divine form, a draught of ecstasy entered my heart—more and more and again more, until I couldn't hold it and the tears streaked down my cheeks in utter joy. I didn't even want to leave the kitchen to go to bed.

The next morning, when the swami walked into the kitchen, he smiled at me. He said, "You are going to Washington tomorrow. We need you to do PR."

Like Gadhi, one day I was a kitchen *wala*, sleeping in a dormitory, and the next I was back in public relations, staying in a private room in an ambassador's mansion and sleeping on a bed with twenty decorator pillows.

◆ ◆ ◆

THERE IS more to Gadhi's story. After eight years as king, he finds his tribal wife standing before him in the royal hall. She has come to ask the king what she should do about her missing husband—and, seeing Gadhi, she shrieks, "*You* are my husband!"

Everyone sees this as a travesty. Gadhi's subjects feel they should cleanse the dishonor of living under a tribal king by spilling the king's own blood. Again people gather in the city's great square. This time Gadhi stands on a scaffold with a thick rope looped around his neck. Once the trap door under his feet is opened, he will drop. Gadhi closes his eyes . . .

When he opens them, he is standing at his bathroom sink, looking at his own face staring back at him in the mirror. Gadhi walks into the next room and checks his bedside clock. The events that have seemed to encompass sixteen, maybe twenty years of his life have taken place in ten minutes. He hasn't even missed breakfast.

When the swami told Gadhi's story, he invariably followed it by saying the only way to avoid being trapped by the play of the mind is to meditate, to go deep within yourself.

I could see the sense in that. Meditation can help us identify with the reality that underlies the blaze and thunder of our lives. Yet I don't like to think that Gadhi made the wrong request. I don't think that instead of asking to understand the world, he should have asked for immersion in his innermost self.

Certainly such a request would have bypassed the drama, saved us all a lot of time and trouble. But did Gadhi really have that choice?

I know I didn't.

14. ❧ The Foolish One

ON THE HEELS OF IVAN, I met Terrence. We were in Florida, about a dozen of us, living in a rented house in Coconut Grove and preparing for the swami's upcoming visit to Miami. My role on an advance crew was to contact the media, write and deliver news releases, arrange for interviews, distribute posters and fliers, and then be helpful in any other way I could. Usually I arrived about a month ahead of the swami.

I was somewhat fuzzy about the roles others played, the people who found the venues, for instance: who set up the events, who got the posters printed, who purchased supplies. Terrence was one of these people and had figured in an earlier tour the swami made to the United States several years before. Longevity like that carried a certain clout among the staff: those who had met the swami on his first tour, who had been to India, were more relaxed than the rest of us. For them, this world was at least a bit familiar.

I had come to the house in Coconut Grove that morning, having driven from Atlanta with someone who had a car. I was standing in a large solarium just off the kitchen, drinking a cup of chai.

I heard a man's voice behind me say, "So, you've just arrived." I turned and saw him enter the room. Terrence moved with ease, even grace, but there was nothing larger-than-life about him in a physical sense. He was tall, slender, fair, freckled; he had regular features. He was attractive, but you had to look hard to notice. There was, however, a certain power in his focus, and this I felt immediately.

My reply was a brief "yes," and though I knew his observation was an opening for me to say more, the words didn't form. For those few minutes that we spoke, I felt the full weight of this man's attention. He asked about my background, my experience of the swami, how I'd ended up on this tour. As I answered his questions, I felt as if the two of us were standing together inside a snow globe, only instead of bits of sparkling pseudo snow, we were immersed in his perceptions. I watched myself as if through this man's eyes, thinking, *Nervous . . . awkward . . . predictable . . . needy . . .*

I *was* all of those things. I knew it. I hated this about myself, and I wanted to say to this man, *I don't like her either. She's a clumsy fool. I want to be like you. I want to be self-assured and centered. I want my voice to sound easy and mellow, like yours does.* But, of course, I didn't say any of this. I spoke predictably about myself, I saw the initial spark of interest disappear from Terrence's face, and all the while I wanted to be him.

I think that's what infatuation is: wanting to *be* someone else. I didn't understand the depth of my self-desertion in that moment, how devastating it was for me that I felt more empathy for this judgmental man than I did for myself. What if those were Terrence's thoughts! Even so, I didn't have to own them. I didn't have to care. And I *did* care. I so wanted this man's approval.

◆ ◆ ◆

SHORTLY AFTER THE swami arrived in Miami, Terrence was sent ahead to someplace else, and later I went in advance to yet another place. For the next several months the swami's tour hopscotched across the continent. When he reached the West Coast, the swami set up a permanent ashram, and his entire tour staff stopped and settled there for almost a year.

This gave the swami a chance to impose a regular discipline of meditation, chanting, study, and service on the ragtag crew of would-be yogis traveling with him—and it gave me a chance to see Terrence. I had a writing project that took me into the kitchen, where he offered *seva*, and within weeks I had made him my idol. Then, for the thousands of hours I could have spent in other, more beneficial ways, I thought about Terrence.

Everything I'd learned from the swami in New York about disciplining my mind was gone. I wasn't chopping in the kitchen now. Amid my current *seva* assignments, this kitchen project and PR, for much of the day I was alone in my room, sitting on my bed, writing. Anyway, I was supposed to be writing; what I was actually doing was concocting delicious fantasies.

I had indulged in romantic fantasies in my early teens. Tall, awkward, and bespectacled as I was at the time, fantasy was my only option for romance. Now, in the restraint of the ashram, I found that romantic fantasies were once again my outlet—and the powerful atmosphere gave them a heavenly appeal.

I would have a conversation with Terrence in the kitchen about the project I'd been asked to undertake—this was something that interested him as well—and often I walked away feeling foolish. Back in my room, I'd replay that scene and the perfect replies would shimmer in my mind—uplifting sentiments with cosmic overtones, cleverly phrased, amusing— and with them, a feeling of palpable, pulsing love would course through the whole of my physical body. *This is divine*, I'd think. I thought it was love, but, of course, I also knew it was infatuation.

The word *infatuate* comes from *fatuous*, which means *foolish*, but that's mild reproach compared with the reality of the state it describes. Infatuated, you live in a tiny, airless mental world of imaginings in which you—but it isn't really *you*; it's a *perfect* you— in which the perfect you is in perfect harmony with whoever happens to be your animus of the moment. The unutterable joy of these romantic fantasies is then balanced by the pain that comes when you see the object of your affection in the flesh, weighted down as you inevitably are by the expectations spun from your own fantasies.

The next time I saw Terrence, I would be awkward, tongue-tied, slack-brained, and Terrence would be . . . well, whatever he was, which was uninterested in me. I would resolve this anguish when I was next alone, by figuring out what I should have said, should have done . . .

The ersatz love that came up when I thought about Terrence in the privacy of my mind was an elixir I didn't seem capable of giving up. Yet dealing with the reality of Terrence afterward was a down-spiraling agony of self-consciousness, self-effacement, self-abasement, self-reproach, self-condemnation, and self-loathing.

One morning I had an especially painful exchange with Terrence in the kitchen. Half an hour later, I worked out that I'd misheard what he was saying, and went back to the kitchen to let him know I now understood. He wasn't there. "He's gone to his room," someone said. I found out where that was; threaded my way through the ashram's labyrinth of hallways; knocked on his door; and, when he opened it, said without preamble, "I thought what you meant was . . ."

The look of surprise and annoyance on Terrence's face hit me like a splash of icy water. I was mortified. If I could have disappeared in that moment, that's what I would have done. Instead, I swallowed, put some context around what I was saying, and apologized for my interruption of his quiet time—a serious breach of ashram etiquette, especially coming as it was from a woman to a man. Terrence was aware of my feelings for him—he'd have to have been asleep not to be—but my arrival at his door was a blaring declaration that I had been thinking about him nonstop since our last conversation, for him a nonevent that had happened more than an hour earlier.

◆ ◆ ◆

THERE WAS another factor that complicated my response to Terrence. I'd had some mysterious experiences while chanting. One moment I was swaying in time to the chant, thinking blissfully of Terrence, who was playing the tambourine just a few yards away, and the next moment I was sitting motionless, goggle-eyed, looking around to see if I could fathom who, if anyone, was responsible for the pleasurable but disconcerting experience of having another consciousness enter mine during the chant. This was a subtle event, but still, it was an event.

The first night this happened, I decided I needed to ask Terrence if he had anything to do with it. If so, I was going to ask him to stop. The next day, I told him I wanted to talk with him and asked if we could go for a walk. Though he agreed, he obviously felt the need to set some boundaries.

"This is not a relationship," he said before we had rounded the first corner behind the ashram. "There is nothing for us to talk about. There is nothing happening between us except in your very active mind."

He went on like this for five or ten minutes, and I listened, taking it in as if it were medicine. When he finally paused, I said, "I guess that means you don't have anything to do with the experience I've been having."

"What do you mean? What experience?"

When I explained what had happened, he sounded relieved. "Oh," he said. "You've just had your first out-of-body experience."

It was more an *in*-body experience, but I wasn't going to quibble. It was embarrassing to speak with Terrence so frankly about this, especially after the verbal lashing I'd just received from him. Once he realized what I'd wanted to ask him about and why I was confused, Terrence spoke to me like a big brother about subtle energies and the heightened awareness a person feels around a spiritual master.

I only half heard him. I felt numb, and the next morning, my body ached as if I'd been beaten. I knew it was related to my conversation with Terrence. But why? I understood later that by taking up an extremely sensitive topic with the object of my infatuation, I was opening myself to him even further, giving him greater weight and more power in my life—when I'd already given him way too much.

I was having mysterious experiences with a spiritual practice. Why hadn't I taken my questions to my spiritual guide? Why hadn't I asked the swami?

◆ ◆ ◆

BUT THEN ONE day, during a chant with the swami, I closed my eyes and offered up a question that no mature spiritual seeker would ever ask: *Why me? What did I do to deserve this?*

As they say, we have only to ask . . .

In my mind's eye, I see a Native American warrior in traditional dress. He is tall, with bronze skin and long, dark hair, braided, I think, wearing a headdress with a single feather. As I look at his face—he has an arrogant tilt to his mouth, angry eyes—I have an intuitive understanding, this is me; I am looking at myself, at my own soul housed in a body that was my vehicle in a previous lifetime.

The idea of past lives is something I used to laugh at before I met the swami. There are so many more people on Earth than there have ever been before. If we're just being recycled, where did all these new souls come from? I never raised that question with the swami, and after a while I was grateful I hadn't. In a spiritual tradition that views every cockatoo, cockroach, and blade of grass as a form of consciousness, "new" souls will never be in short supply. If any vestige of my earlier views of reincarnation were left, it dissolved in that moment when I closed my eyes and recognized myself in buckskin and beading.

I find myself looking out of this warrior's eyes into the upturned face of a woman. She is pleading with me, speaking soft, placating words—words she doesn't mean. Underneath her words is the message don't hurt me, *and this she communicates with every movement of her head, every tremor in her voice. Her weakness disgusts me. I reach out and slap her face.*

We cut to another scene: Still in warrior form, I am standing on one of the huge glacial rocks strewn across the American plains. Two women in conversation walk past the rock, below me. The two of them are twittering together like birds. They're weak, looking to each other for support, and the sight of them nauseates me. There is a waist-high rock beside me. I get behind this smaller rock and roll it off, onto the women.

I opened my eyes then, in shock. In the sweet, safe darkness of the chanting hall, I thought, *I'm getting off lightly.*

The swami, sitting some five yards away, playing his tambourine and chanting, turned to me and nodded.

So, there was more at play in my obsession with Terrence than was apparent on the surface. I didn't know specifically what this vision meant—was Terrence the woman I had slapped? One of the women I had killed? I didn't know and didn't care. What was apparent, what I could actually *feel* whenever I thought of this vision, was the fierce and fragile consciousness of that being who was driven to violence by his fear of fear. What poetic justice it was that such a soul would take birth in the body of a woman who was nervous around men!

Pertinent and thought-provoking though this information was, it didn't change the dynamic I was involved in. Then one day, the swami offered me some overt help.

◆ ◆ ◆

IN MY PR role, I appeared on a local television talk show as part of a panel discussion on nutrition. I was the token vegetarian. One of the other panelists was a Roman Catholic nun who said, after the show, that she would like to meet the swami. I invited her to lunch at the ashram and afterward introduced her to the swami as he sat outside in a shady little courtyard in front of his residence. The swami took the opportunity to speak about the beauty of monasticism and the power of his own *sannyasa* initiation in India. He described the radiant sunrise as he, free of all worldly ties, took a ritual bath in the river. Turning to me, he said, "I'm going to tie you to these colors one day." Then, looking concerned, he added that he'd have to shave my head.

It was the first time I'd heard the swami say anything about giving monastic initiation to a Westerner. Sitting six inches from him as I was in that moment, I felt drenched in *shakti* and tolerant of any possibility the swami might suggest for me. When I got back to my room, I burst into tears.

The swami had always said we didn't need to leave the world in order to know God. Recently, he had started conducting marriage ceremonies for some of the staff. The kitchen manager had married the head of the construction crew; two people on the advance crews had married; more couples were forming every day. Others on the swami's staff would be able to lead normal lives, with relationships and good haircuts and beautiful clothes, and I was going to have to become someone weird, someone in monastic orange with a shaved head. It was grossly unfair.

After a few minutes, I pulled myself together. Why have a guru if I was going to ignore his instructions? This was a clear directive, and surely it was in my best interest to open to it.

The next day I asked if I could speak with the swami. I was invited to a private *darshan* in his quarters. I took with me as an offering my makeup, all of my pocket money, and the few pieces of jewelry I had. He gave me back the makeup.

I told the swami I understood that he had probably brought up this matter of *sannyasa* as a ploy to vault me out of the sex and marriage fantasies I'd been living in recently.

The swami laughed and began talking about a woman who had been one of his *darshan* secretaries until a few months before. While she was traveling with the swami, Jyoti had been married to another of the swami's devotees, a businessman in New York. While she was away, Jyoti's husband found a girlfriend, and then Jyoti returned to New York to divorce her husband. Now Jyoti was back in the ashram, and she wanted to marry another man. "She's a nice girl," the swami said. He paused, and through my mind went the words *but dumb*. He went on, "What

I don't understand is why she would want to go through all of that again."

The swami was not, I understood, talking about Jyoti. Although Jyoti's second marriage did ultimately echo her first in the very feature the swami had pointed out, what he was bringing to my attention was the disintegration of my own marriage. In the *darshan* with Tom, the swami had spoken about how the bonds of marriage are forged through a couple's relationship with God. Now, he was inviting me to contemplate my failed marriage as an expression of my own karma, my destiny, the price I must pay for having lived in certain ways. Viewing my issues with marriage in that light, I knew I wasn't going to resolve them simply by choosing a husband who was on the same spiritual path.

Did I want to go through that experience again? Not really.

❖ ❖ ❖

ONE AFTERNOON, alone in my room, I was pulled into an interior space. My eyes closed, my head dropped forward, and I heard an inner voice: *Up to this point, the experiences you've had with Terrence have been the result of your karmas from past lives.* There was a pause, and the voice continued, *Your experiences from now on will be the result of the way you have lived out these karmas in this lifetime.*

I was creating karma right now! That was interesting. And horrifying. Without my either reaching out to Terrence or running away from him—and without fantasizing about him—I continued to feel the same ache of inadequacy and longing whenever I saw him for another two and a half years.

By that time, we were in India.

15. ᴄᴠ "Little, Little, Little"

THE FLIGHT FROM NEW YORK to India had an epic quality; it was so long it seemed to span an entire incarnation. Counting the commutes to and from the airports, layover time in Europe, waiting at customs, and the interminable sitting, sitting, sitting on the plane, the trip took more than fifty hours. That may sound inconsequential compared with what seekers from the West once had to undergo in looking for an Indian spiritual master—traveling by sea and overland, through the mountains of Afghanistan and Pakistan. But flying is enough. Anyone who makes the trip sacrifices some part of himself in it.

About fifty staff arrived in India ahead of the swami. We were to help prepare the ashram for his arrival. He would come with several hundred more devotees from New York, whose flight the swami would join at the end of his European tour.

We landed in Mumbai at about three in the morning. The steamy, end-of-monsoon air softly brushed my face, and the warm, smiling brown-eyed faces offered, "Madame, your bags . . . Madame, come with me . . . Madame, Madame . . ." I had no fear, no sense of being in an alien land. I felt at home, listening to the sound of the melodic Marathi language around me while I sucked a mango drink through a straw.

A smaller, advance crew had left New York a few months earlier and were at the Mumbai Airport to greet us. They were ecstatic to see us, grinning widely, their eyes afire with *shakti*. Their bodies, however, were emaciated. Several of them had bright purple splotches between their toes and on their hands and elbows. "It's nothing," one of them said, in response to a hesitant query. "Just a little fungus." Actually, the purple dye was to combat the fungus, which was less visible on its own but which, if not dealt with, would itch and spread.

We arrived at the ashram as the sky began to take color from the rising sun. The countryside was dark and silent, and the ashram turrets rose in the early-morning light like a peach-colored palace. When I stepped through the threshold arch, it was the realization of a personal dream. I could hear the morning chant from the temple; the measured rhythm of sacred syllables laced the air with holy sound. We were ushered past the chanters, through the small courtyard, and into the dining hall, where three long mats had been unfurled on the stone floor. We sat in silent rows and drank hot chai from bright orange plastic cups. When our eyes met, we shared smiles. It was too wonderful to contain.

◆ ◆ ◆

IN THE AFTERNOON I explored the ashram gardens, and, walking down a shaded pathway lined with life-size statues of Indian saints, I heard a caterwauling come from a building about fifty yards away. It was a concrete structure the height of a two-story building with bars across the entry. Standing in the doorway was a large bull elephant. It's considered auspicious to have an elephant in residence at an ashram, and I had heard about the existence of this animal long before I got to India. Still, seeing him like this was a surprise—not only behind bars but chained as well.

The male elephant is beset by an annual condition known as musth, in which testosterone rages through his system and he becomes violent toward not only other male elephants but any creature. For a moment I listened and watched in wonder. I was silent and motionless and standing some distance from the elephant, but he became aware of me. He stopped his cry and turned to look at me. I knew, under his scrutiny, that this animal detested me and that had he not been forcibly confined, he would have killed me. I could feel malice radiate from him like a burning heat.

The swami once said the elephant had been a yogi in his last life. He had performed some meritorious action, or perhaps it was just his attempt at yoga that had brought him the merit, and this was why he now lived in a sacred place. He had fallen from yoga by acting on burning sexual desires. He had probably been a monk, as well as a yogi, because his fall had been precipitous. As a result, he now had the body of an animal: specifically, he had the body of a male elephant, a creature driven by lust.

Standing under the elephant's malevolent glare, I had the inexplicable thought that I might have been a part of his past-life drama, possibly even the cause of his fall. Whether or not it was true, this was one animal I did not want to be close to. I thought, *Okay. I'll stay out of your way*, and I turned and began walking away. The elephant started to bellow again, and now, instead of directionless frustration, his cry took on new animus. His fury was focused on me. Just before I left that part of the garden, I turned back to look. The elephant was still watching me.

◆ ◆ ◆

CHANTING BECAME, once again, painful. My knees hurt as they had when I first sat for chanting and when, months later, I held a *tamboura*, an Indian stringed instrument about the size and shape of a small tree and made from a pumpkin. Now I was sitting in half lotus on a marble floor, padded only by a thin square of white wool and a piece of linoleum, which the Indians called "carpet." I felt as if I were undergoing torture on some medieval rack, and on top of that, I was often wet with perspiration.

We were in postmonsoon, a steamy heat. It's not an environment most human beings voluntarily choose, but it is, I found, the ideal habitation for insects. There were no screens on the ashram windows at that time, only iron grillwork to keep out animals. When we chanted before dawn or after sunset, the lights in the temple drew all manner of flying things. I would sit in quiet agony, chanting in Sanskrit, and look up to see a moth with the wingspan of a hummingbird fly past my face. The place was thick with insects. Many were harmless, but not all. And by the time I felt tiny feet landing lightly on my arm or ankle or on the back of my neck, it was too late: the predatory mosquito had struck.

In New York, the swami had once spoken about Indian mosquitoes, telling us that while our mosquitoes in America were big, an Indian mosquito was much better. An Indian mosquito is smart, the swami said, and he's fast. I'd laughed then, but I wasn't laughing now, sitting in the evening chant, swatting away squadrons of these devilish, airborne stinging machines. Smart and fast, indeed. I began to dislike chanting. The only practice I looked forward to was meditation, when I could sit in the darkened meditation cave, swathed in a shawl, sweating, perhaps, but safe from aerial attack.

We also protected ourselves as we slept. In the women's dorm, we strapped sticks onto the bed legs, and these sticks, standing several feet above the bed, were draped in mosquito netting. We left the netting up during the day, because the trick was to make sure when you lay down, the mosquitoes were outside the net and not trapped under it, with you. With these thirty-five netting-swathed beds in neat rows, the dorm looked like a sea of cocoons or an array of disembodied spirits. Both of these metaphors reminded me that I was in India for the sake of *sadhana*, a path of spiritual preparation.

When the swami had first moved to this spot in India, he lived in a tiny thatched hut, so he was affording his disciples a more comfortable living space for *sadhana* than he himself had enjoyed. He was, in a sense, coddling us. At the same time, I found myself dumbfounded by the simplicity of my life. How could it be that my possessions had been reduced to the contents of two wicker baskets small enough to rest under my cot? A few cotton garments, a clock, a framed photograph of the swami—that was it.

◆ ◆ ◆

OUR CREW had come in advance to help repair, scour, and polish, and this we did, individually and collectively, in the various projects we were given. I cleaned the courtyard shoe rack of its moldy contents, made whisk brooms with string and straw, disposed of rat remains each morning on the dormitory steps, painted a planter a pale apricot for the swami's courtyard, and, once—my favorite task—helped a friend polish silver and brass in a meditation hall in the upper garden. This was in a building where the swami had lived years earlier, while his present quarters were being constructed. The hall held an enormous, age-darkened painting of the swami's own guru, attended by a wealth of metal objects: candle holders, lamps, trays, and other accoutrements of worship. Bhavani, who was a skilled carpenter and printer, as well as a poet and musician—she kept a zither under her bed—also knew the best way to polish metal.

"You read the directions on the label," she said, stopping me from my random application of various cleaning solvents. "These folks want their products to work, so they tell you the best way to use them." This meant the silver was polished with a great deal of paste and a lot of effort, while the brass got a thin film of solvent, which was allowed to dry before we buffed it lightly with a dry cloth. It all worked. Polishing metal is a paradigm for following the spiritual path: you receive instructions from one who knows the way, and, using your own God-given common sense, you follow the instructions. Would that I had understood this at the time.

Three weeks before the swami was to arrive, a crew of about twenty was assembled in the ashram's new *mandap*. A *mandap* is an outdoor pavilion, and this one was roughly half the size of a football field. Pillars held up the roof, and the whole enclosure was surrounded by a half wall, like a ledge, into which was embedded iron grillwork, like an elaborate fence. This *mandap* had been constructed while the swami was away and finished several months earlier—finished, that is, except for one vital detail. The iron had not been sealed, and in the monsoon rains, it had rusted. Our crew was to sand and repaint it.

"By hand?" I asked. "We're going to do this by hand?" Yes, we were.

Surrender is an elegant yogic concept that was often invoked in the ashram. In Western terms, to surrender is to give up, to be defeated—you might surrender gracefully, but still it is understood that by surrendering you have lost the battle. In yoga, surrender is a matter of accepting what is—not holding out for what you imagine something to be or want it to be or feel it ought to be but allowing it to be as it is. The benefit of yogic surrender is sweet contentment. I had many opportunities to explore surrender when I first arrived in India, but this—sanding the fence around half a football field—was the most compelling.

We were given three grades of sandpaper. Initially, we would go over an area with a grain so coarse that, were it a beach, you might call it pebbled. This removed the rust. The next two grades of sandpaper prepared the surface, making it smooth again so it could be painted.

I started off in the southwest corner, and my first approach to the work was one of total ownership. Since I was sanding a fence, I was going to sand it well. I put my attention, my energy, my power of will into preparing that fence magnificently. And I was successful. Within hours, the crew supervisor was bringing people over to my little corner, saying, "*This* is the way it should look."

This ambitious phase lasted for about a day, and then it ended. I lost interest in building my self-esteem through sanding, and I entered a social phase. I was sanding between two men, one of them quite attractive, and I found myself trading life stories with them, amazed at how urbane it sounded to have been in the press in Hawaii, to have lived in a valley where the rain fell every night, to have interviewed the swami . . .

The social phase lasted somewhat longer than the first, a couple of days. Then I was just sanding. There was nowhere for my mind to go, nothing else to take my attention. I was in the *mandap*, with the others, working my way around the seemingly endless length of iron fencing.

In the beginning, we were in the *mandap* for six hours a day. Soon it was apparent that at this rate we wouldn't finish in time, and so we were there for eight hours. Then nine. Then ten. As the swami's arrival approached, it seemed we were doing nothing but the *mandap*—and it was then that I received a graphic demonstration of the benefit of making such an offering of effort.

I realized I needed a tool that was on the other side of the *mandap*, and so I got down from the ledge where I'd been working and walked across the pavilion floor. As I walked, I could feel the cement under my feet. It was smooth and cool to the touch, like something silky, and I enjoyed the sensation of my foot hitting the ground—the heel, the ridge along the outer side, the ball of the foot—and then pushing off again with the toes. My whole body felt good moving through the air. I enjoyed the feeling of my arms swinging gently on either side. I could sense the distance between the top of my head and the roof. There was a delicious feeling of space, as if I were moving through a cathedral.

It was a divine experience, and, finally, I noticed I was having it—I noticed that walking across the *mandap* was one of the most ecstatic experiences of my life. I wondered why. And then it struck me. My mind wasn't focused on where I had been; it wasn't focused on where I was going. My mind was totally with me, walking across the *mandap*. It was pure bliss.

◆ ◆ ◆

FOR ASHRAM MEALS we all came together in a space larger and grander than most Indian temples and with songbirds flying in and out freely through the open windows. We sat in long rows, women on the garden side of the hall, men on the temple side, all of us chanting a *namasankirtana* while servers walked up and down the lines, ladling enormous helpings of food. Once the serving was finished and a rousing mantra rang through the hall, many people performed private ablutions. I would repeat the mantra eleven times, as the swami once said his own mother had taught him to do before eating, and I would sprinkle water three times clockwise around the plate. The latter was not for supplication but to establish a moat that would protect the food from the army of large black ants that roamed the dining hall floor.

At night we ate on rimmed metal trays, called *thalis*, when the meal was likely to be rice with a bean dish as thin as soup. At noon, when the food was more substantial, we ate on broad, flat leaves stitched together with tiny twigs. The rice, cooked vegetable, and two chapatis (a thin, circular flatbread) were served on this leaf plate; the dal (like a bean soup) went into a tiny stainless steel bowl, called a *wati*. The Indian village women who ate with us would pour the dal onto the rice, which they could do easily without spilling any because they would ask for and receive a pile of rice, in some cases two hands high. The village women, particularly, would hold their thumb and third finger together and jab at the plate again and again with staccato demands that the server pile it high with rice.

I was accustomed to thinking of rice in terms of a serving of one scoop, an ice-cream scoop, and the extravagant interest of these village women for what I'd always thought of as filler food astounded me. I had to stop myself from staring, from nudging the person next to me and indulging in the luxury of a moment's shared amazement. The village women were as thin as pencils. I learned that they did heavy work, construction jobs that entailed carrying wet cement in flat metal bowls balanced on their heads, often climbing with these bowls of cement two or three flights on bamboo latticework up the side of a building. They worked like this from dawn until late afternoon, and because they were fortunate enough to be employed in the ashram, their wage, which was low but higher than the local norm, included this very lunch. For many of them, I suspect, it was their only meal of the day.

In the dining hall, everything was served twice. After we had been eating for five or six minutes—never as long as ten—the servers came through again. I began to see that beyond what was offered at the two servings, the village women never asked for additional vegetable or dal or chapatis. Sometimes the Western women requested more of the vegetable, called *bhaji*, and the servers would usually give it, but their faces registered surprise. I surmised that in India it is permissible to ask for rice, the staple, the foundational food. Everything else is offered to you in the amount the host feels that he can safely serve and still ensure that everybody eats.

The other side of this custom, the side that most dramatically affected me, is that Indian hospitality requires the host to offer as much food as he can. In the scriptures of India, the guest is God. This meant that the dining hall servers took delight in heaping our plates with food. I would hold up my thumb and index finger a quarter of an inch apart, saying "*tora, tora, tora*"—"little, little, little"—and watch in dismay as a beaming Indian man shoveled enough rice onto my plate to feed, from my perspective, four people for a week. I would put my hand out over the plate, palm down, signifying "no seconds on *bhaji*, please," only to have him, with a mischievous grin, sneak the serving spoon under my hand from the side. He wasn't being malicious. He was, according to his own culture, being gracious, generous, caring. He was letting me know that I could eat.

In fact, I *had* to eat, because there was an ironclad policy in the dining hall that it was unacceptable to throw away food. This policy was enforced, and it had the full weight of the guru's intention.

So I did eat the food, but after a while, it became apparent that what I couldn't do was digest it. Rice, beans, potatoes, bread: it was like taking in a load of cement. The food would go into my stomach and stay there. For hours. For days, it seemed. When it finally left my stomach and traveled to the nether regions of my digestive tract, it created noxious gases. Other than this, nothing left my system.

Weeks went by in this way. At first, I didn't think about it; I didn't even notice. Then I thought about it a lot. I asked a few questions. I tried hot water. I tried ayurvedic remedies: bitter, waxy black pills that had to be chewed before they were swallowed. The solution came in the form of diarrhea, which was, initially, a great relief. But very soon that gave way to disbelief—how much shit could a body hold?—followed by dismay. The purge was far more painful and dangerous than the ailment it cured. I wasn't experiencing the result of laxatives; this was from giardia, intestinal parasites.

This was the reason village women could down a mountain of food each day and still have bodies like pencils: most of what they ate nourished the microscopic life forms that colonized their digestive tracts. It was happening to me as well. This was not an uncommon ailment, and it had an inexpensive fix: take a course of Flagyl. I, however, decided, as an act of renunciation, that I would not spend money on medication. I would take care of my unwelcome guests the native way—by eating only what these tiny life forms did not themselves like to consume: rice, curd, and ripe bananas. It was a rigid regime because, of course, after a short while, I didn't like those foods either. Why would I do such a thing to myself?

◆ ◆ ◆

THAT DAY IN the United States when the swami spoke to me of *sannyasa* was my introduction to the idea of living as a renunciant. My notions of what that meant, however, did not come from the swami. He often said that all a yogi needs to let go of in life is her false identification. Forgetting this, I took my instruction from one of the Indian men on staff—a former postal inspector who had left a wife and daughter to take vows in a more traditional ashram than the swami's. After the swami's public statement to me, this man told me that being offered *sannyasa* by one such as this particular, and very special, swami constituted an obligation. "To turn down such an invitation," this man said, "would mean no chance of liberation—in this or any other lifetime." He loaned me a booklet on monastic life that spoke of begging for food from a limited number of houses and not handling money. I decided what this would mean for me was living with austerity and without consideration for material possessions.

In India, one afternoon I found my way to the meditation hall in the upper garden. The late-afternoon sun was slanting through the windows, turning airborne dust motes into floating sparks of brilliance. I was alone in the room. I sat cross-legged on the floor, directly in front of the large picture of the village saint who was the swami's guru, staring at his radiant dark form until my vision altered and the figure began to glow and pulled away from its background as if his form were in bas-relief. Inside, I heard a roar of energy like a strong wind, and my back began to arch.

At first it seemed little more than a postural adjustment. But once I noticed it, the motion became stronger. I found myself being moved, as if by an omniscient hand working inside me. My back arched, and the trunk of my body was drawn gracefully, ineluctably forward until my forehead came to rest on the linoleum floor. The movement was not a collapse into comfort, as was often the case when my head dropped forward in meditation; it was an offering of myself, a bow.

As it turned out, this was one of the pivotal gestures of my life, not the physical posture, per se, but the words I put around it and, specifically, the meaning I later gave those words: *I promise I will put* shakti *before everything.*

It was a vow. It was a pure gesture, inspired by my experience and expressed through my understanding of renunciation. It is difficult to fathom all that flowed out of that moment, the pain and torment I later put myself through.

I promise I will put shakti *before everything.* My extreme stance prompted me to refuse to spend money—a pittance—for Flagyl.

As we worked longer and ever longer hours on the *mandap*, I fought with myself at every meal. What should I eat? What was too much? What *were* the right foods? I figured it would all become clear once the swami arrived.

16. ∽ Crowned

THE DAY THE SWAMI RETURNED, It seemed that the whole universe converged to greet him. There was a massive reception at a hotel near the airport. I was one of the ashramites invited to attend this reception, which was unfortunate. There were long banquet tables filled with rich foods, the likes of which I had never seen: *bhajis* (fried vegetable fritters) with chutney, *sira* (sweet pudding), *gulab jamun* (spongy milk balls in rose-scented syrup), *barfi* (milk and cashew sweets wrapped in silver), and so much more.

I gorged myself on these treats. On my first eye contact with the swami, as we headed back to the ashram, I felt slightly queasy. I was in the back of a large van, looking out the back window, when the swami's car pulled up behind us. He was sitting in the front on the passenger's side, and even though I was seeing him through two vehicle windows and his dark glasses, I could clearly perceive his eyes boring into mine. It was a warm look, an accepting one, but I knew there was a lot yet to come.

During the first few months after the swami's arrival, there were many *bhandaras*, feasts, with fried foods and rich sauces and sweets. Such foods are the antithesis of the dietary tactic I was taking to deal with my intestinal parasites, which thrive on rich, sweet food. I was supposed to eat only simpler foods that are said to limit the bugs' virulence, numbers, and life span. It is difficult for me to gauge the effectiveness of this rice-curd-banana treatment, because I found it impossible to follow.

I had rarely if ever eaten Indian feast foods. I wanted to taste them, and I was unable to sit in the dining hall, eating rice and curds, when interesting, yummy-looking dishes were being served to everyone else. Of course, I would ask for just a little and then some oily delicacy would be heaped on my leaf plate. God, if only I'd taken nothing at all. Because, as I've said, I had to eat the food—and then I'd be sick again and would lose more from one end than I'd put into the other.

I began to perceive that I was losing weight because of my gluttony. Some people later pointed to this as a sign that I was crazy, or at least seriously illogical. A person loses weight because she doesn't eat, not because she eats too much. It's a physical law. But sometimes I couldn't eat at all because earlier I had eaten too much, or too much of the wrong thing. When I tried to explain this, people would get a certain look on their faces, and I would know that I was talking too much about food again. It was easy for that to happen. I talked about food a great deal because I thought about food almost constantly.

I'd ponder what the right foods were, and the right amounts. A friend and I used to split breakfast in the ashram coffee bar: a bowl of spiced cereal and a bowl of yogurt was too much, but half of each mixed together was, for me, the ideal breakfast. While my friend worried about gaining weight, I just didn't want to eat too much. Of course, I was the one who thought of the arrangement, talked my friend into it, and made sure it happened, and the one who was bereft on the mornings when the supply of curd was low. Even if we arrived in time for curd, I didn't like the idea of taking one of the last bowls of it, because then other people would have to go without that day. It felt like I was stealing food, taking the curd out of someone else's mouth so I could stuff it into my own.

Glutton, a little voice inside would say as I took curd from the dwindling supply. *Pig*.

This inner monologue became even more critical when I actually overate, or ate something terribly wrong. Like *sira* or *gulab jamun*.

Eating again? You are so stupid. You are an animal. When are you going to learn? What does it take? Is it too much to ask of you? Have a little discipline. You haven't digested yesterday's lunch, and here you are, eating sweets. You pig. What did you come here for? To eat?

I know now that the problem lay not in what I ate or didn't eat, but in these astonishing, venomous insults that I heard going on in my head. They were spoken in a distinct voice, inside my mind. I thought it must be God. A wrathful God. An all-seeing and all-powerful God from which there was no escape. I thought it was the guru, attempting to lead me, and that I wasn't strong enough to follow. It didn't occur to me that I was my own inner critic, that these same poisonous insults had been going on my entire life just below the level of my awareness.

There was, at the same time, a great deal of *shakti*, of pure power, in my life. It seems unlikely that anyone else thought of me as undisciplined. I got up every morning before three, put on a sari in the dark; I meditated every day for an hour or two, worked for maybe five hours, chanted for fully five and a half. There were moments of ecstasy in the day; I was often in a state of supernal joy by the time I went to bed. But there was a gnawing concern as well, and in time that is what grew, the anxiety; it deepened and intensified and stretched. Something odd was happening—that much I knew.

◆ ◆ ◆

AFTER I'D BEEN in India for about ten months, the swami announced that he would bring to the ashram a ranking official, from the Sarasvati order of *sannyasins*—the order to which the swami himself belonged—and have this dignitary initiate several of the Western men as monks. One of the ashram women felt that women should be included in this honor and put a sign-up sheet for *sannyasa* on the bulletin board in the women's dorm. I added my name to the list without a moment's thought. I was living as a monk anyway, and promising to continue doing so didn't seem like such a radical step.

It *was* a radical step, and, in retrospect, it's astonishing that I would have asked to take a lifetime vow of celibacy, poverty, and total submission to divine will without even pausing to reflect: *What will this mean for me? Is it the right direction for the rest of my life? Is this the time to make a commitment of such magnitude?* My failure to ponder these reasonable questions made signing that list not so much a gesture toward light as a profound act of self-denial, an attempt to erase myself.

What kind of monk would I make, when I still couldn't keep my eyes off Terrence? Whenever I saw him walking in the garden, I felt a twinge in my belly, as if I were being incised by a shard of glass. If he were at a safe distance—say, a few hundred yards—I'd watch him for a moment. Even though I couldn't make out his features, I took pleasure from seeing the grace of his movements. He had the responsibility of looking after a pony, and he walked that pony around the ashram as if it were a huge, playful dog. In my mind, they were the perfect pair—and better than I was. Every time I saw them, I would make that same soul-destroying comparison. There seemed to be nothing I could do to stop myself in this, but I could take a vow of celibacy. I could promise to myself that I wouldn't act on my desires.

There were twenty-three women who made the request for *sannyasa*. The list was duly presented to the swami, who announced that instead he would give us all *brahmacharya*. This was a lesser commitment in that we could still own property and hold jobs. We were vowing celibacy, as well as promising to "speak softly" (to use no more force than is necessary) and "speak the truth" (to hold the highest Truth above all else in your life). It was a little like becoming an apprentice swami, and we were to wear a color as well—yellow.

A couple of days before our initiation, I talked with one of the other *brahmacharya* candidates, a lovely young woman who had arrived in India just a few months before. She told me that she knew the vows were a perfect step for her because she was passionately in love with one of the men who was taking *sannyasa*. "I can see us," she said, "on the same path, walking side by side toward God, serving God together."

I was horrified. I mulled this over for about three hours, before going to one of the senior monks planning our ceremony. I told him, "Some of the women on this list haven't been doing *sadhana* very long. I'm not sure that everyone knows what they're getting into. I don't think they can even conceive of what it is to make a commitment like this."

He probably knew, though I didn't at the time, that I was also speaking of myself. This monk took my question to the swami, who met with the *brahmacharya* candidates in his apartment the day before the ceremony. The swami was as sweet as a grandfather, speaking in a voice that issued from so deep that I felt I might be back in the womb. This is a lifetime commitment, he told us. Do not take it lightly. Then he added that if at some time we found we wanted to be released from the vows, that would be all right. We should come to him and tell him, and it would be fine. We should not, however, dishonor the vows.

As I heard the swami speak, I knew that I hadn't been asking about this other woman at all. I was the one who hadn't been doing *sadhana* very long—three years only. I was the one who didn't know what I was getting into.

The initiation was much more than I'd envisioned. The ceremony itself is ancient, and it involved venerable Indian disciples, some of whom had their own ashrams elsewhere. We were given necklaces with beads the size of golf balls; the *palu* of the sari was pulled over our head and a secret mantra whispered into our ear. But more than the ritual was the energy that accompanied it. Walking away from the open-air pavilion where this initiation took place, I felt I had been elevated. The woman before me, also a *brahmacharya*, caught the sunlight, and, watching her walk in her yellow sari, I felt as if we must be about to merge with the sun itself.

◆ ◆ ◆

THAT WE WORE only yellow turned out to be initially challenging. None of us had known that this would be an aspect of our new life until a couple of days before we entered it, so most of us spent the first three or four months of *brahmacharya* with only one yellow polycot sari to wear day after day after day. I washed out the sari in a bucket every night and hung it on a line at the bathhouse, and it was dry the next morning. It was ready to wear, but after the first few weeks, I wasn't ready to wear it. I didn't mind wearing yellow, but still I wanted more than one garment. Finally, one day I got into Mumbai and found a couple more yellow saris and—to my delight—a long shirt, called a kurta, and some pants, both in yellow cotton.

A few days later, I saw the elephant on the street in front of the ashram. I had successfully avoided him all this time. Whenever I saw him being led into the crowded courtyard in the afternoon, I would sit at the back, and in the mornings, when he made his daily promenade through the ashram and down the street, with two ashramites sitting on his back and chanting a sacred text, I stayed far away from them.

On this day, after ascertaining that the elephant was being led away from me, I looked around and caught a glimpse of a man who had just arrived from Hawaii walking into a chai shop across the street. This man, who was quite attractive, was not just from Hawaii but also from the Hawaii media. While I'd never met him before, there was a good chance he would have news of familiar politics and people.

It was a delicious opportunity: I had the perfect excuse to have chai and gossip with a man—and I didn't have to do it in a sari. I could get out of the six yards of fabric I was wearing, out of the infernal floor-length petticoat, and into something comfortable, something in which I felt almost hip. I raced upstairs to the dorm, tore off my sari, and pulled this new outfit out of the basket under my bed with more excitement than I have ever had about any garment in my life. I let my hair down, not hanging on my shoulders, which would have been viewed as obscene, but held back in a band at the nape of my neck—the way I'd worn my hair for years as an ordinary person. That was the way I felt in this outfit: like a regular person.

I charged downstairs and into the street. It doesn't take long to drink a cup of chai, and I didn't want to miss this opportunity. I was stopped short. I felt the elephant before I saw him. Oddly, it was like an embrace, and I knew immediately what was happening. I was being held by a huge, warm, soft, flexible limb: the elephant's trunk. I had made a serious miscalculation. I was in such a rush to get across the street to this guy from Hawaii that I hadn't noticed I had darted right in front of the elephant.

I was as good as dead. In that moment the half thoughts, questions, and understandings that flashed through my mind had the weight of revelation. Why hadn't I looked again for the elephant? This was a malevolent and vastly superior force. There was no point in struggling. Yelling wouldn't bring help. No one else *could* help me. And since there was nothing I or anyone else could do, I consciously relaxed. I took a deep breath in.

That's the last thing I remember until I came to. I found myself lying flat-out and facedown on the filthy street. I was still alive! But if I didn't move fast, I might not stay alive. I rolled away from the elephant's feet and, without a word to anyone, ran upstairs to the dorm. Thinking that God must be telling me to fear for my life if I wore pants or drank tea with a man, I tore off those clothes, put the sari back on, and wrapped my hair into a tight little bun on top of my head.

One of the ashramites who was on the elephant's back approached me that afternoon to make sure I was okay and to ask me, on behalf of the mahout, the elephant's keeper, if I would please not tell the swami what had happened. The mahout was afraid he'd be in trouble. I had my own reasons for not wanting any attention on the incident, so I agreed not to tell—though this, too, was a mistake.

Less than a year later, the elephant attacked the mahout, who, unlike me, was injured almost to the point of death. It seems that for the mahout, I was a warning he failed to heed.

For me, the contemplations continued over the course of years. I began telling myself that what I'd needed to learn was to look both ways before crossing the street. Or to watch out for elephants that are fallen yogis. Then, twenty-five years after the event, in the course of my ashram service, I read an interview with someone who had witnessed the incident. From him I received truly pertinent information. This man described how the elephant picked me up and threw me, full force and headfirst, onto the street. From what this man said, I bounced on the street on the top of my head. I asked him about it later, just to be sure. He told me that the carpentry crew had a private name for me after that day—the Flying Banana—and he said, again, that he'd watched me bounce on my head. "It was like you were in a protective bubble of *shakti*," he said. "Nothing was going to hurt you."

I feel certain that's the way it happened: I was saved by a miracle. I wish I'd thought more about it at the time. What I always focused on was the murky undercurrent of the event: the dangers of being caught by desires of any kind, the incendiary nature of lust, the furies that it raises. Like Gadhi, I was crowned by an elephant, but in my case it seemed the animal was trying to annihilate the animal in me.

◆ ◆ ◆

TERRENCE WAS TO be married—and to another *brahmacharya*. When I first heard this, I was relieved. Thank God it wasn't me doing this stupid thing. Later, a large group of us from the ashram were on a *yatra*, a pilgrimage, with the swami in Central Maharashtra. We were in Nashik that day, and I ignored the formal itinerary and went to the town's storied temple to Lord Rama. I sat in a back corner of the temple, and my whole life began to unravel. The thought of Terrence came into my mind—by then he was just weeks from the wedding—and it occurred to me that I had loved this man. Perhaps I loved him still. How could I know? I had consciously closed him out of my mind. I'd shoved him from my heart. Now he was about to marry another woman, and I would never be able to explore my feelings for him.

One thing I did know: I was no monk. This was a charade, this thing with the yellow costume. I could go through with it if I wanted to, I could go through my entire life playing this game, and then I would come back for another lifetime, or more, so I could experience whatever it was I needed to experience, whatever it was I was running away from right now in my yellow sari.

While these thoughts warred in my mind, I wept. I sat in the corner of the Rama temple and sobbed. Wild, ragged cries were coming out of me—when the swami walked in. I caught a flash of orange as he strode past me. He had a retinue with him, as he always did, but it was just a handful of people, not the hundreds who were on this *yatra*.

I didn't stop crying right away, but the swami didn't turn, didn't look at me. He walked straight up to the *murti*, the statue of Rama, and began doing worship. He wrapped a shawl around Lord Rama, offered incense. When I was breathing normally again, I joined the group at the front of the temple. The swami led us out to the front steps, where, he said jovially, he had slept on a number of occasions. He chatted for a few more minutes and then walked to the temple garden, telling most of us in the group that it was time now for us to be on our own.

I turned, and there was Terrence with his bride-to-be.

I congratulated them, and we spoke for a few minutes. At one point, as he often had done in the past, Terrence questioned the wording of something I'd just said. What did you mean by that? What are you trying to say? That's not the right word at all.

It was the kind of thing that used to tie me up in knots. Now it didn't.

"Maybe it was the wrong word," I told him. "Maybe I should have said . . . Oh, I don't know. What would you have said?" So what if I'd made a mistake. Did it matter? Not to me. He was just another person by then, and what a relief that was! What difference did it make to me if I didn't measure up to his standards? I don't know at what point it had happened. Perhaps it was all those months of spiritual practice. Perhaps it was having faced it squarely moments before in the temple. Whatever the cause, I was free of my obsession with Terrence. I was free.

I went off shopping with his fiancée, looking for yoga paraphernalia, which was cheaper and easier to find in Nashik than it would be back in the United States, where we would soon be going—she as a bride and I as a *brahmacharya*.

17. ⌒ Eat a Little More

PEOPLE BEGAN TO COMMENT on my lack of physical substance. A man I'd met on the swami's US tour arrived; after a welcoming hug, he pulled back by an arm's length and asked, "They don't feed you here?"

Someone tutoring me on a talk I was giving told me I should not say that meditation makes you lighter. "They'll wonder if you're going to disappear right before their eyes."

One morning I examined myself in a mirror. My face had always been thin, but now it was gaunt, and this was accentuated by a yogini bun: the hair pulled up tight against the scalp, secured with a rubber band, and twisted into a tight roll on the top of the head. What most amazed me, though, was the light in my face, blazing from my eyes. My eyes were pools of energy. I looked a bit like a witch—not Glinda the Good Witch, my first role model from my first big-screen movie, at age four. No. I looked like the Wicked Witch of the West. I paused in front of the mirror long enough to wonder, *Is this what I want?*

But I wasn't about to turn back. I'd embarked on my noble experiment. I was following the swami's path to liberation, and I was determined to see it through.

Later, I dreamed I was walking across water on a long bridge. The bridge was on fire, the flames whipped high by a wind that caught my sari and made the fabric billow in the air like a flag. In the dream, I was heading into certain death, but because I didn't know what else to do, I walked on.

The day after the dream, the swami called for me. I had to climb a flight of stairs to reach him, and I couldn't make it up the stairs in one go. I had to stop on the landing to catch my breath. I felt as if I were ninety.

When the swami saw me, he started yelling: What kind of yoga was this I was involved in? Yoga brings *shakti*. It brings power. I was like an old woman.

He told me my new *seva* was to get strong, and he sent me to the infirmary, where I was given a plasma transfusion. Lying on the cot with a needle strapped to my arm and the chill of fresh fluids entering my body, I felt tremendously relieved. I was being taken care of; I was going to be all right.

Of course, it wasn't that simple.

Later that afternoon, I was driven to a hospital, a small but immaculate facility owned and operated by the swami's own physician. I was given a room with another American ashramite, Shankari, who was recuperating from pneumonia. Dr. Patil explained that in Indian hospitals, it's customary for the family to provide a patient's food, to live in the corridor outside the patient's room so that they can cook for him; otherwise, the patient doesn't eat. Dr. Patil said that because he knew my family was far away, his wife would cook for me while I was there.

Dinner arrived shortly, served on a metal *thali*: dal, vegetables, chapatis, and a mountain of rice. "Oh, I can't eat the rice," I said to the young woman, a servant, who had brought the tray.

Apparently, she didn't speak English. She looked blank and left without replying.

"Why don't you just leave what you can't eat," Shankari said.

I ate around the rice. When that was all that was left on my tray, I saw Shankari pick up a clump of rice the size of a large apple and take a bite out of it. She was an unassuming woman, her brown hair pulled back into a neat ponytail, her eyes observant. She noticed me watching her, and when she'd finished chewing, she said, "I like rice. I like the way it tastes on its own. Rice has its own very delicate flavor."

I looked again at my own plate with its mountain of rice. It scared me. I hadn't eaten rice for months. Rice felt like lead in my stomach; it gave me gas; it inspired a battery of insults in my mind. *Pig. Glutton. Don't you know you can't eat this!* But Shankari was eating rice, and I knew that nothing bad was going to happen to her because of it. Maybe it would be all right for me to eat *some* rice. I picked up a lump the size of a *small* apple and bit into it.

The rice tasted like nectar in my mouth, but the sensation of chewing that mouthful of rice had nothing to do with flavor. I experienced love flowing through my body. My inner response was riveting. It was like the rice was *prasad*, a divine gift. I ate it all, every grain, and went to sleep that night in a state of ecstasy.

◆ ◆ ◆

GOING TO SLEEP in ecstasy was not unknown to me. In the ashram, chanting five and a half hours a day and ending the day with a forty-five-minute invocation of Lord Shiva, I often fell asleep in a state of joy. It wasn't until the next morning that I knew that something momentous had happened. Before I even opened my eyes, I realized that I was awakening in joy.

For a moment I lay still and relished this unaccustomed gift: morning bliss. Gingerly, I raised my eyelids, propped myself on one elbow, and looked around the darkened room. For a moment, I didn't remember where I was. Oh, yes: Dr. Patil's hospital. I could see from the bedside clock it was three o'clock. Time to get up. I walked through the dark to the bathroom, still in a state of mind-stopping ecstasy.

I drew a bucket of water for my bath. It flowed from the faucet like a sacred river. The act of pouring that water over my body was a sacrament, a devotional rite. Yet to see that body! My poor body. What had I done to it? The spindly arms! I could count each rib! I'd emaciated myself in pursuit of the experience I was now having—an interior love that had nothing whatsoever to do with the austerities I had endured to invoke it.

I laughed, I wept, and for the next couple of weeks I walked through the world with a sense of unconditional joy. I was in a constant state of love. I treasured this feeling, monitored it minute by minute, something I had never done before in my life. When my experience of love seemed in danger of diminishing, I stopped whatever I was doing to sit on my bed, lean against the wall, repeat the mantra, and focus my attention inside on that astonishing font of *shakti*. Because of that inner power, everything in my life changed.

I ate normally but paid little attention to the food. I was absorbed in looking at the world through new eyes. As a matter of taste, I'd always preferred muted colors: earth tones. Now I found that the brighter a color was, the more alive it seemed. Mrs. Patil offered us a choice of new bedsheets, and I reached right past the apple green to a vivid orange-yellow-pink floral print that, to my eyes, radiated *shakti*. The colors themselves seemed to carry feelings, to beam goodwill. I believed I was perceiving a level of reality that had been hidden to me.

One afternoon on a walk, I heard a dog barking, and when I turned to look at the mangy, wiry street mutt, I thought the dog was laughing. A village man in a white dhoti walked up behind me in that moment and started yelling at the dog. The man's face was contorted, and I saw that, for him, the dog's barking was painful. In effect, the man himself was barking, filling the air with the sound of his own rage. I could see that in that moment we, this man and I, were each creating our own reality. Our respective mental states gave us wholly different experiences. For the two of us, that one barking dog was in two different worlds. For years I'd heard the philosophical tenet "you create your own reality." Now it was my experience, a message coming to me through my senses. Revelations came minute by minute; it seemed the whole world was my text.

The day I left the hospital, Dr. Patil told me, as far as he could see, there was no reason I couldn't eat. There were, unfortunately, some reasons his medical tests couldn't detect.

My sugar addiction and social fears kicked in again once I

was back in the ashram, and this sense of joy began to dissipate. It was a gift I couldn't hold, and at the time its loss was a source of guilt for me. My mind wasn't stable enough to sustain such a state. I had been elevated into unconditional joy as a reprieve, a chance to transcend my wildly self-destructive mental conditioning, if only for a few weeks. And the experience came, I'm certain, as an act of grace. Of course, the very notion of grace evokes questions. Whose grace? How is this grace given? And why?

My consciousness seemed suddenly to have expanded through the swami's direct intervention. How that happened, I can't say, but I can think of no other explanation for it. Obviously, it wasn't the rice.

◆ ◆ ◆

THE SWAMI SENT me back to an ashram on the West Coast of the United States, where I could find foods my body was accustomed to, where I might receive nutritional or psychological help if I wanted. I didn't do either. I told myself I was going through a yogic process. But by this time I'd lost that elevated state, and before long I was back to my old should-I-or-shouldn't-I agonizing over food choices.

Some family friends who were in the neighborhood showed up at the ashram one day to take me to lunch. They knew I was vegetarian, and they could see I needed to eat, so when they left, they gave me a basket of fruit. "Keep it in your room," my auntie told me. "That way you'll have something if you're hungry at night."

It was a lovely, thoughtful gift, but my experience upon receiving it was a palpable heaviness. The fruit itself weighed on me. I didn't want this pile of food—to be eaten at will—sitting in my room. It might pull me, like a siren song, into doing something that would make me very, very unhappy. I might eat it all, or eat so much of it that my stomach would feel leaden and my inner critic would throw verbal knives at me. I gave the fruit basket to the ashram kitchen.

Those friends didn't stop with the fruit. They called my parents that night, and the next week, my whole family—Mom, Dad, my brother, his wife, and their eleven-month-old daughter—arrived for a visit. My mother wanted me to come home. "I'll feed you," she said. "You'll gain weight." The thought made me nauseated. I remembered being a skinny kid, leaving for school each morning with a "good" breakfast: eggs, bacon, toast, and a malted milk drink that made me feel like gagging.

My family, too, left me with a basket of fruit, bigger than the first one. That, too, I gave to the kitchen. I stuck to my own style of eating: not eating.

One day I decided that for lunch I would have an apple. It was a beautiful piece of fruit: red, shiny, not too big. Using a paring knife, I cut the apple into precise quarters, removed the core with the seeds in it, and ate one quarter. It was filling, that piece of fruit. I ate another quarter. Quite filling. I could feel the food in my belly. For now I'd eaten enough. I wrapped the rest of the apple to save for later. Or give away. Other people could eat more than half an apple, but I wasn't among them. I didn't want to risk the inner retribution.

◆ ◆ ◆

AROUND THIS TIME, someone in another US ashram, not the swami's, died of starvation. A spate of newspaper articles on anorexia appeared, and the ashram's director and board took notice. How could they not, when there I was, standing before them: a poster girl for dietary deprivation!

A high-level meeting was convened to consider the situation I posed. For obvious reasons, I was not invited to attend. I was told afterward that if I wanted to remain at the ashram, I would need to agree to accept the community's help. I had to check in with a psychologist, I had to undergo a battery—another battery—of medical tests to ensure there was nothing physically wrong, and I had to agree to eat. Specifically, I was to move across the street from the ashram, into the apartment of a young woman I'd never met, who had agreed to share every meal with me. It was quite a fall for one who'd recently thought she had attained a high state and was going through a yogic process of purification. But I wasn't. By then, even I knew it.

I took the tests, talked with a doctor who specialized in eating disorders, and heard from her, as I'd known I would, that there was no physical reason I couldn't eat. I told her about the plan: how I was eating with this woman, focusing on protein shakes, and ignoring my inner directives. The doctor must have approved of the plan; she didn't offer one of her own. As I was leaving, she said, "Good luck!" I heard a lot of feeling and content in that brief message, but at that point I wasn't aware of how much terrain I had left to cover—and how few are successful. Only one in three anorectics fully recovers; one in ten dies within ten years. The death rate from anorexia is twelve times higher than any other cause of death in young women.

As I went into this new phase, I repeatedly heard a refrain singing in my mind: *It's one, two, three strikes you're out at the old ball game.* It's a cheery little ditty, but, thinking it over, I found the message chilling. This was my second strike, the second time I was being saved. I had just one last chance. If I missed this time, I'd be "out." It made perfect sense. I'd weighed ninety pounds when I came from India; now I was eighty-five. There was no more weight to lose. I hadn't had a menstrual period for two years; my body had been in survival mode for quite a while now. I had to get it right this time.

By slavishly following a regime set by someone else—which turned out to be a challenge for us both—I put on the weight everyone required of me. To me it looked like inert flesh. I was the right size and shape, but everything about me was leaden. My inner intuition may have been irrational, wild, off-mark, it may have been crazy, but it was mine and the only inner connection I had. I had to shut it down for a while just to survive, but if I didn't find a way to live with that voice, life itself wasn't going to be worth much. When the swami showed up at this ashram, on the initial leg of another Western teaching visit, there was less attention on me, and I started listening again to the voice in my mind, following what seemed to be higher guidance from within. I started eating less.

Rather than cutting down portions, which would have been noticed, I skipped meals. The only time I could get on a transcribing machine, which was necessary for part of my *seva*, was during breakfast, and that seemed a clear indication that breakfast was an unnecessary meal. Then one night, after eating a particularly hearty dinner, I had a vaguely repugnant dream about sex, and that was my cue that dinner should be eliminated as well. After a few weeks of this, I was starting to lose weight again.

◆ ◆ ◆

MY SOLUTION WAS to seek guidance from the only authority that, at this point, I trusted: the swami. I asked and was told I could talk with him the next day as he made his daily rounds of the ashram departments. It was in the lobby but at a quiet time. Perhaps twenty people were around. I was nervous approaching the swami. He was laughing with someone; when he looked at me, I heard inside, *What now?*

I told him I'd been losing weight again, people were worried about me. In fact, no one had said a word to me; I was worried. I knew this voice that was telling me not to eat was crazy . . . or I thought it was probably crazy. I wasn't sure. It might have been the voice of God, too, and if it was that, then I didn't want to ignore it. I figured the swami could lay this issue to rest. I would bring it up and listen very carefully to what he said. Of course, he would tell me that I should eat more, that I should eat a lot more. He'd said it before.

What he said this time was that I could eat a *little* more—emphasizing "little" by holding up his forefinger and thumb with about an inch of space between them. I felt abandoned. What did he mean by that? I had no idea.

A woman who was in the lobby that morning told me later that the swami pointed his index finger at me as if he were scolding me or at least making a very strong point. She said he told me I needed to smile more.

"You were very serious," the woman said.

That I was. I am certain the swami gave me that instruction, but I wasn't in a frame of mind to hear it. I was listening for him to tell me to eat more. At that point I was craving those words from him, even as I was craving food. Craving food, thinking about food, meditating on food—and not giving myself permission to eat.

It was crazy. But not nearly as bizarre as what happened next.

18. ᴄᴠ The Crow and the Coconut

LIFE AROUND THE SWAMI settled into a familiar routine. On tour, there were nightly programs in which the swami spoke on the teachings, led us in chanting and meditation, and gave *darshan*. *Darshan* is a Hindi word that means "to see" or "to be in the presence of," and it refers to the tradition of approaching a holy person or sacred icon for a personal moment. Often this is only a glance, but it's also a chance to ask a question or make a request, and to receive blessings. When the time came for *darshan*, almost everyone in the room, at this point several hundred people, would join a line in the center aisle and "go up" to the swami's chair for his *darshan*.

Less than a week after my encounter with the swami in the lobby, I was bringing my head up from a bow in that evening's *darshan*, when he leaned over and said, through his translator, "They need an ashram manager in Hawaii."

I sat back on my heels and looked up at him, perplexed. "Does the swami want me to go?"

"They really need a manager," he said.

The following week I was on a flight to Hawaii—and to an entirely new role.

◆ ◆ ◆

MY TRAVELING COMPANION was a tough merchant marine named Balaram, who was to be the ashram's new cook. We hardly spoke on the flight. He worked on menus and cooking flow charts, and I . . . I didn't know what to do. In my last *darshan* with the swami, I'd asked him if he had advice for me. He smiled and looked past me, saying, "Learn to manage an ashram."

I was nervous, and I had a right to be. Here I was—a reclusive wordsmith with serious food issues and dressed neck to hem in yellow—being sent to a small, residential facility where I would be welcome hostess, program manager, volunteers coordinator, rules enforcer, facilities supervisor, and bookkeeper. Rather than words, I would be dealing with people, schedules, objects, and money. At that point, I'd never even balanced a checkbook!

The new management team, Balaram and I, were led by a program director who was one of the new Western swamis and (fortunately!) an old friend. The population of this tiny ashram expanded and contracted like an accordion: eight ashramites one month, twenty the next. Some would come for a few months, or a year, or longer; others were there for a few weeks or even just a few days. And, too, there were those devotees who came to the ashram to offer *seva* or attend a class or *satsang*—sometimes 150 for a large celebration.

These people were fascinating and luminous beings: the tree-trimmer who regaled us at breakfast with tales of his dreams from the night before, the lawyer and his wife who moved in with a preadolescent boy who was more than they (and I!) could handle, the city policeman who left his guns on the shoe rack when he dropped by in an afternoon for a few minutes of meditation, the airline stewardess who wanted a more nourishing lifestyle between her flights, the former sea captain who had been fired for turning around his ship midcourse . . . In fact, each of these people wanted a new direction in his or her life. Collectively, they *were* the ashram; they were the reason for the ashram's existence.

My part in the operation required both a skill set and a subtlety that I was stretching myself to develop, and I remained nervous. My desk, the ashram's operation central, sat at the front entrance, right beside the table and small refrigerator that served as Sugar Central—candy bars, soft drinks, ice cream. I began pounding down sweets. This is something that can happen with anorectics: from a terror of food, suddenly I manifested an addiction to sweets. To Balaram's intense annoyance, I still didn't eat the meals. There was no room left for dinner when I'd just knocked back four maple-glazed pecan-sesame bars, two Wha Guru Chews, and a handful of Tofutti Cuties.

For the first time ever, I became overweight. I, who had cut through my life like a knife, was suddenly displacing air when I moved; I felt like a massive ship, a barge. But more than that: in the quantities in which I was eating them, these sweets were poison to my body. Eating like this was as self-destructive as not eating.

Something had to change.

◆ ◆ ◆

IN THE *Yoga Vasishtha* there is a brief story. A crow lands on the frond of a coconut tree. A coconut falls and, in some versions, hits the crow and kills him.

That's the story. It's often abbreviated even further: the crow lands; the coconut falls.

In the West, where we customarily look for cause and effect and where our entire scientific tradition is built on finding an accurate account of causality, this story is sometimes seen as an example of how our actions bring a particular experience to us. The crow's landing on the tree is thought to have caused the coconut to fall; the crow's death is seen as a direct, though inadvertent, result of his own action.

In the Indian tradition, even with its acceptance of the law of karma—which is a subtle and mysterious form of cause and effect that says your motivations bring particular results to you— there is much less interest in physical causality. The point of the story is that the crow lands in the path of a falling coconut and, being in this spot at this very moment, the crow dies.

Much of what happens to us, whether we see it as destiny or as the play of pure chance, occurs for us in the way that falling coconut hits the crow: as a surprise. The swami used to say that the power of meditation burns up the vast reservoir of karmas we carry inside us. Out of this reservoir of karmas, he would say, at birth we have already extracted a portion to "drink" in this lifetime, and those experiences we will go through. No matter what, those particular coconuts will fall. It's the nature of the human experience: into every life coconuts must fall.

The issue isn't *why* a coconut comes at you but how you handle yourself when it does. Like my experience with Terrence: I had been destined to have difficulty with this man. He was a falling coconut—and anorexia was an even bigger coconut, a humongous coconut. If you're in a good mental state, sometimes it's possible to duck. I think that's what the swami was giving me a chance to do from my miraculously elevated state. When you can't duck, what you can do, always, is to watch yourself deal with the coconut. By continuing to seek a solution in a seemingly unsolvable situation, you will find that a new and useful perspective can come to you. This is what happened for me with anorexia. It's my belief that meditation—and chanting and contemplation and service to a higher cause and, yes, grace— created the space inside me that allowed me to step back, so to speak, and truly see myself in this circumstance. Seeing myself clearly, if only for a glimmer of a moment, I could begin to make other choices. I'll describe two of those moments.

◆ ◆ ◆

A MIDDLE-AGED WOMAN stayed for a week, and several times while she was there, I went on an afternoon walk with her. She seemed like a gray person: she had brown-gray hair, she spoke in soft, dove-like tones, and her skin had a grayish pallor, as if she'd had all the life ironed out of her. On her final day, she told me she'd recently been in a mental institution. Our conversation was long.

The woman said she'd had a lesson she had to learn. In the mental institution, she realized it was the same lesson she'd always needed to learn. She saw she'd been given many, many opportunities to learn that lesson. Each time she'd refused to learn it, she had ended up going into a more difficult circumstance. The lesson never changed, only the circumstance in which she had to learn it. Once she was in the mental hospital, she said, she could see that she was the one who had made it necessary to be there.

"What I had to learn never changed. I could have learned it earlier, but I didn't. So I had to learn it in a mental ward. Being there was not a pleasant experience." She paused. "I wish I hadn't done that to myself."

She never said precisely what her lesson was. I never asked. I didn't need to. I was at that time up to my neck in my own lesson. As I listened to this woman, I saw that I, too, would surely end up in a mental institution if I didn't learn my lesson. But what was this lesson? I really didn't know.

That was the first moment.

◆ ◆ ◆

THE SECOND CAME not long after. One of the men who lived in the ashram was like a brother to me. The second time I ever saw Dan, when he arrived at the ashram in India, in my mind I heard an exultant voice saying, *My brother is here!*

In Hawaii, he was working as a teacher in one of the community schools and, from my perspective, giving me support at the ashram. He got together a hike for some of the ashram children—there were four or five at the time—and invited me to join them. I was quite excited about this. Hiking is something Tom and I used to do, something that always rounded my corners a bit, but I hadn't been for a walk on a forest path in years.

We left right after lunch, walking through the lush rain forest in the foothills of Mount Tantalus. It was like stepping into a celestial realm. We walked past stands of fragrant wild ginger and hibiscus, through a forest of guava trees that looked like massive sculptures, and under tree ferns we could have used as umbrellas. Green was all around us, and, even amid the children's laughter and ricocheting energy, there was a sense of peace.

After the first hour, one of the children suggested that, since this was so much fun, we should expand our original plan. Why stay at the base of the mountain? We could go all the way to the top, to the very edge of the volcanic cinder cone!

The idea gained immediate traction. We were explorers, after all; we were yogis. We had to go to the top of the mountain. We had to, and I had to. I couldn't put a damper on the children's adventure. And at the same time, I knew very well that I wasn't prepared for a climb. I didn't have the clothes for it, I didn't have the shoes, and, most of all, I didn't have the muscle tone!

Long before we reached the top of Tantalus, my feet were blistered, my flaccid body aching. By the end of the afternoon, my every step was an act of personal will. At one point I thought, *This is hell!* Then it struck me: we were back on the easy terrain. Just a few hours earlier, this same forest had seemed like heaven to me. The trees had looked like friendly beings, the flowers had been exquisite, the path inviting. What was different now? These were the same trees and flowers. It was the same path. I was performing precisely the same action on that path: I was walking. The only difference was the way my body felt—and who was responsible for that? I alone had made this body. I was the one who'd chosen to eat as I had, who'd chosen to remain sedentary.

◆ ◆ ◆

THAT NIGHT I spent hours thinking this through. I was sitting in the ashram meditation hall when it finally struck me: I'd been doing all of this to find God. I didn't need to find God. God knew very well where I was, and anytime he wanted to, God could find me. In the meantime, what I needed to do was take care of myself. That was my whole responsibility: to take care of myself.

This is an oversimplification. There were lots of little moments that went into supporting this revelation—and it was exactly the same revelation I'd had in Dr. Patil's hospital. It brought back to me what that woman fresh from the mental institution had said: the lesson had never changed. The variable is not *what*; it's *when*—when, finally, are we going to surrender to what is?

I had recently read *The Tibetan Book of the Dead*, the text that Buddhist priests chant as a guide to the soul during the period immediately following death, to describe the progression of choices the soul will encounter. These choices come up at graded levels of experience, beginning with the beautiful and ending with the horrific. There are specific and intricate descriptions of options presented to the soul, from the dazzlingly brilliant blue light, the most fundamental form of God, all the way down to the blood-drinking, wrathful deities that come bearing nooses and wearing garlands of human heads. Despite appearances, the choice is always the same. Each time the soul chooses comfortable delusion over the more stark and startling reality, that soul moves into another level of experience, each successive level being less appealing than the one that preceded it.

The other point I took from *The Book of the Dead* is that whenever the soul does make the right choice, she is freed.

I decided to take care of myself. I made a pact with myself that every day I would take my body for a walk and feed it three balanced meals. No matter what.

It was a good beginning. It took about two years of truly disciplined eating and exercise before I could undo the negative mental habits I'd adopted. There were uncomfortable moments, times when I was nervous about what I should or shouldn't eat, but because I'd actually contemplated that moment of truth, I was able to hold it.

Something else I contemplated was the swami's role in this healing. The swami, knowing I was barely feeding myself, had sent me to manage an ashram. He could have sent me away— back to my family, anywhere but inside his own organization. Instead, he gave me a semipublic role that was, for me, quite challenging.

He knew that in learning to manage an ashram, I would have to learn how to manage myself.

◆ ◆ ◆

I CAN'T SAY that I ever truly finished with anorexia—any more than one could *finish* with any addictive behavior. A psychologist explained this to me once, and his explanation made perfect sense to me.

I was seeking guidance on another matter and was telling this psychologist about myself, filling in the background he had no way of knowing. I said, "And I used to be anorexic—that was years ago, in my midthirties."

"If you were an anorectic," he said, "it started a long time before that."

"Well, yes. All through my twenties I was fanatic about not weighing more than a certain amount—"

"And long before that."

"I suppose that's true. In my teens I was never really in touch with my body." I once saw a school record in which the nurse reported my visit to her office one day to ask about losing weight, even though I was "not at all overweight."

"Before that."

I paused to consider: just when *had* I taken in that voice from hell: the nagging, you-can-never-do-enough-to-satisfy-me critic that seemed to live inside my mind? It certainly had aspects of my mother. I had memories of Mom asking me at fifteen, "Why can't you be little and cute, like Terry?"—the five-foot-two blonde who was my best friend. I had no answer, no solution to my gangling awkwardness, but at least I could make sure there wasn't too much of me. I wouldn't get *fat*. But the voice must have come from someplace deeper. Why had my mother's words lodged in me in that particular way? My brother had grown up in the same house; he'd never stopped eating.

After a moment's silence, the psychologist said, "And it's not over. It isn't something you went through in the past, and now it's just a part of your personal history. Anorexia is a tendency not to take care of yourself, and if you've ever had the tendency, you will always have the tendency. You're doing very well with it now. . . ."

I would *always have the tendency.* I think it's the most useful piece of information about anorexia I've ever heard: I would always need to watch how I'm nourishing myself.

19. ❧ The Next Step

IT WAS MY BIRTHDAY, and Sue, one of the ashramites, insisted that as her gift to me, she wanted to take my shift on the front desk that afternoon so I could spend some time at the beach. The ashram in Honolulu was maybe three and a half blocks from Queen's Surf, the very beach where I had once spent my weekends in a bikini, where I'd drunk beer and tequila, where I'd thrust my hand into the ocean and come up with my wedding ring. What would I do there now? I didn't have a bikini; I didn't have a bathing suit of any kind.

I tried to articulate my lack of enthusiasm for this unexpected outing, but Sue was not to be put off. "Oh, come on, "she said. "It's your birthday. You shouldn't be sitting at the desk on your birthday." More for her sake than for mine, I found something in my closet that approached sports attire and left her at the ashram's front desk while I trudged to the beach.

It was early afternoon, and the sun was relentless. I was wearing yellow cotton pants and a kurta, and I was hot. What was I going to do at the beach, anyway? I couldn't swim in this outfit. This was the birthday treat the universe was giving me. It occurred to me that it was really too little, too late. I had been managing the ashram in Hawaii for almost three years; this was one of my rare afternoons off, and I wasn't even spending it in a way I wanted to. Someone else had picked my outing for me and sent me off on it—alone!

Was this supposed to be fun? What was I getting from this

life, anyway? Why was I doing this? Was it really necessary for me to be living in an ashram? Did life have to be this extreme?

Involved as I was with my thoughts, I didn't see the woman coming. She walked right up to me on the sidewalk and took hold of my closest arm with both of her hands. "You," she said, looking straight into my face with her luminous eyes, "are a nice woman. You are a very nice woman."

She was probably about sixty—gray-haired, unkempt, uncombed, and hung with cloth bags, but she wasn't looking for money. She'd just wanted to tell me that.

"Thank you," I said to her. She smiled at me, disengaged herself, and walked on.

That was it. That was my answer. What I was receiving from my service in the ashram was just that: I was becoming a nice person.

I sat on the beach for the next few hours and, watching the gentle waves of Waikiki, considered how I was undergoing deep purification. The swami had once said that each of us had come to the ashram in order to receive something—"something to take with you when you leave," he said; "something you can eat along the way." I now knew what he meant. Shadows were leaving my mind, making room for more light. Even the way I'd let Sue usher me out the door was an example of this: the person I was years before, when I was coming to this same beach to party, was never very gracious about accepting a gift she didn't want.

At the end of the day when I returned to the ashram, I found that it, too, had been transformed: the meditation hall was festooned with balloons and tissue-paper flowers and a huge HAPPY BIRTHDAY sign the ashram kids had spent the afternoon making. It was a complete surprise, the party. And it was lovely. Someone took a photo of me that evening: no makeup, hair undressed, the plainest yellow clothes you can imagine—and a radiant smile. That was what I was gaining from my time in the ashram: there was a lot more room in me for joy.

◆ ◆ ◆

No makeup, hair undressed—and a smile

AN ATTRACTIVE MAN showed up at our little ashram in Hawaii. He was tall, blond, educated, a few years older than I. He moved into the men's dorm with a big photograph of his own guru, his stories about life in South India, and a psychic sensitivity that I found interesting. He'd articulate my thoughts word for word a moment after they went through my mind. My response was to once again experiment with my feminine nature.

One evening this man organized a group of ashramites to go to the movies, and I accepted his invitation to join them. While I was dressing—which yellow outfit should I wear?— I put on perfume. Too much perfume, because I hadn't worn anything like that for years and didn't remember that a drop or two would be enough. When my fragrance and I arrived on the porch, the man smiled. He knew precisely what had happened. I felt like I was twelve again.

There was one night when, meditating alone in my bedroom, I seemed to be coming into some kind of union with God. The energy going through my body was inexpressibly sweet, and I surrendered to what I was feeling, letting it happen, whatever "it" was. The next morning, I knew the author of the experience probably wasn't God after all. This man was . . . *smug* is the word that comes to mind. He was quite sure of himself.

Before very long, I realized this man wasn't someone I wanted to spend time with, but I also figured that if I'd been so very interested in him, I wasn't much of a monk. I telephoned the person closest to the swami, a person who was by now a swami herself and had been formally installed as the swami's successor. I told her I felt it was time for me to leave *brahmacharya* and leave the ashram as well. I told her my savings were almost gone—which was true—and I needed to get a job. She told me to write to the swami, said she would give the letter to him. I heard back almost immediately: a telephone call from one of the swami's secretaries, telling me I had his blessing to go anywhere, do anything, but first I should come to see him. I should come to India.

It took me two weeks to get there—exactly the length of time it had taken me to join the swami eight years earlier. I arrived at the ashram late one night, and the next morning I slept in, listening to the morning chant from a condo across the street, as I bathed, dressed, and unpacked. Later that morning in the courtyard, the swami spoke about how some people come to the ashram without proper respect for its holiness. You act like you're in a hotel, he said. You should be careful; Sunday is coming soon.

He'd give a really fiery talk on Sunday; of this I was sure. That was when his Indian devotees came from Mumbai and Pune.

When the time came for *darshan*, I was nervous about seeing the swami. I was dressed in turquoise, with my hair in a ponytail. What would he say when he saw me? Would he yell at me? I'm sufficiently tall that I towered over the people ahead of me in the line, and the swami saw me long before I got to him. He beamed. When I knelt in front of him, he pulled my head into his lap and stroked my back with his hand while he spoke with the man who was beside me in line. I cried.

When I stood, I was still crying. I walked over to a pillar a few yards away, and, sitting against that, I kept crying. When my tears were finished, the anger came. So it was fine that I'd showed up in turquoise, was it! Fine that I'd written to him and told him I didn't want to be a monk! Fine that I should leave the ashram now and go out to work! If it was fine now, why hadn't he let me know it earlier? He was the one who'd suggested that I become a swami. He was the one who'd been so pleased when I took preliminary vows. He was the one who'd set forward the discipline I was struggling to follow—all the chanting, no movies, no novels, no time for myself. Even without anorexia, it would have been hard, damnably hard. It was the hardest thing I'd ever tried to do in my life. He could have told me I didn't need to do it.

Once my mental diatribe was spent, I heard the swami speak to me, from inside: *If I had told you to ease up on yourself, you would have done it. You're a good girl. You would have done anything I told you to do. And it would have been worthless. You needed to come to it on your own. So, you don't want to know God; you just want to know yourself! Who do you think God is, anyway!*

I wept again.

He was an exceptional teacher. He had sent me to Hawaii to represent him, letting me come, slowly, to the understanding that I didn't need to try to be someone special. He'd told me that already, in a thousand different ways, but I hadn't heard him. To hear that message, I had to say it myself.

When I could, I looked up at the swami and met his eyes for one sweet moment. He rose from his chair, then bowed to a picture of his own guru hanging behind the chair, and walked from the courtyard.

It was the last time I saw him alive.

That night he took *mahasamadhi*—he took the final, great (*maha*) merging (*samadhi*) into God. It isn't that he caused his own death, but he knew in advance when it would come. I heard about it early the next morning. It was Sunday.

◆ ◆ ◆

DAYS LATER, I found the second swami sitting on a tree ring in the courtyard. I approached her, wanting to tell her that she had my support in her new role. I started into it awkwardly, telling her that I felt a lot of affection and respect for her even though I knew we were very different sorts of people, she and I . . .

She looked at me with an expression that said, *You really don't understand, do you?* She pulled my head into her lap and stroked my back—with the swami's own hand. It was his gesture precisely, and, more than that, it was his hand I felt on my back, his all-enveloping energy I felt inside me. Had the second swami even been in the courtyard for my final *darshan?* And if she *had* watched the swami stroking my back, how could she make it feel the same to me?

It took me some days to understand: this experience was an expression of a truth I'd known only intellectually before. The guru is not the physical body, the swami used to say; the guru is the grace-bestowing power of the divine. The guru isn't someone who has power; the guru actually *is* that power moving through a physical form.

I told the second swami I'd had a dream about her a couple years earlier. At the time I'd had that dream, she was traveling with the swami in his entourage, and I was in Hawaii, managing the ashram. The second swami was my physical link to the swami, the one who answered my letters to him and who, when her schedule was too tight for correspondence, picked up the phone and called me. It was she who sent me a scarf on my birthday, who helped me get a box of papayas to the swami, who told me he knew that I'd broken my arm. It was she who conveyed my questions, my news, my requests for his blessings. I'm not sure I thought of her as a person. She was my connection to the universal force I called the swami, but I was surprised to find myself dreaming about her.

In this dream, she and I were standing in the same marble courtyard we were in at this very moment. It was a sunny day, and the light around us was dappled. As the breeze stirred the trees overhead, sunlight and shadow moved ceaselessly across the cream and peach and silver-gray stone. The movement of the light revealed a texture in the atmosphere, giving the impression of a substance heavier than air—weighty and yet fluid, like water. The atmosphere was so thick that we seemed to be standing in an aquarium. Our movements were unhurried, as if we were moving underwater. The second swami turned her head toward me. Seeing me, she smiled. I smiled in return, from inside. Nothing was said, but I knew I was serving this radiant being and we were both pleased.

That I was telling her about this dream in the very spot where I'd dreamed of us being together made us both smile, just as we had in the dream.

◆ ◆ ◆

I STEPPED INTO the courtyard, carrying my laundry bag. I was in errand mode, not particularly aware of my surroundings, but the feeling of the place, the atmosphere itself, stopped me. It was once again as if I had stepped into an aquarium, into an alien substance in which even silence has sound. I stopped in that moment and looked around to see what was happening. The second swami was sitting in the guru's seat, giving *darshan*. By then, the first swami had been interred, but it felt to me as if he were sitting right there before me on the chair.

I found a corner for my laundry and joined those who were gathered around the second swami. I still needed a teacher.

In the first months after the swami's *samadhi*, the second swami began to sit in the courtyard following the evening chant. The lights were off except for perhaps a candle or two, and the soft luminance of the night sky lent a sense of magic to these evening *satsangs*. They would begin with a young woman singing a *bhajan* from one of India's poet-saints in a clear, angelic voice that carried through the courtyard like a bell. The young woman would read a translation of the *bhajan*, and then the second swami would expound on some new way of understanding it, pointing out something subtle that was—at least for me—not initially apparent in the words.

On the first of these evenings, the song was from Eknath Maharaj. I had visited Daulatabad Fort, where Eknath served his guru, Janardana Swami, and I'd always loved hearing stories of Eknath's discipleship. He was a dedicated accounts keeper who stayed up the entire night to find a missing penny in his guru's ledgers, a young man who donned his guru's armor and rode into battle, rather than bring him out of meditation. It was said that he was so steeped in *gurubhava*, in identification with his teacher, that even the guru's horse didn't realize it was Eknath he was carrying into battle and not Janardana Swami.

On this particular night, however, I did not enjoy what I heard from Eknath. The moment the *bhajan* translation began, I was restive with irritation:

> *I would love to be a doorman in the house of a saint.*
> *I would do any kind of work without being told.*
> *Only by serving a saint will I find contentment.*
> *I do not want to do any other kind of* sadhana
> *But to serve my guru, to do his work . . .*

I was looking for another sort of *sadhana*. In my four years as ashram manager, I'd been, quite literally, a doorman in the house of a saint—my desk was beside the front door, and I greeted everyone who entered. This managerial assignment I'd received one night in *darshan* was the most difficult task I'd ever done, and all the while, I had also asked of myself a sort of personal discipline that was neither natural to me nor, as the swami had indicated a few weeks before, truly necessary. I was still sitting on my anger, and it was brought to the surface, simmering, by the words of that *bhajan*.

The second swami began to speak. Her words entered me. I would do anything without being told, she said. I wouldn't wait to hear what the guru told me to do; I would use my own intuition. Looking into my heart, I would see what needed to be done, and then I would do that. I would serve with love—love for myself and love for others.

This is what serving the guru is. *Guruseva* doesn't mean killing yourself in the name of the guru. *Seva* is serving the guru with love.

Her words were like a soothing balm on my spirit. As I listened, I felt lifted out of myself. I could see the last eight years, my entire time with the swami, from a new vantage point. I had pushed myself to succeed in *sadhana*—and my pushing had made it something other than *sadhana*. It was my own ambition I'd been following, and it was that ambition that had given me so much pain—not the swami, not service, not spiritual discipline or the teachings of the guru.

Sitting on the polished marble of the ashram courtyard, I recognized that this second swami was my spiritual teacher. Yet still I mistrusted . . . I don't know what. I suppose it was my own intensity. I was determined not to let my ambition to succeed undo once again my fragile sense of self. While I saw the second swami as my guide in this endeavor, I felt that in this moment I wanted to cut myself some slack.

I left the ashram to find my own way of applying the guru's teachings.

◆ ◆ ◆

BEFORE I LEFT, I saw Terrence's wife. She had just filed for divorce and was now, as she put it, "wiping his footprints off my back."

I was grateful then that I'd never received what I'd spent so much time and energy wishing I could have.

20. ✑ Back to Work

I RETURNED TO HONOLULU, living first with a female friend and then with a male friend, a boyfriend, someone who had been stopping by the ashram in the preceding year, I now discovered, in order to see me. I pulled together a new wardrobe (in black and white), let my hair down, wore mascara, drank wine, and started looking for work. Everything seemed effortless—falling from yoga was one of the easiest things I ever did—except the part about finding work. That was much more difficult than I'd expected. No one I spoke with was hiring just then. "If you can hang on long enough," my former editor told me, "you'll be fine."

Hanging on was, however, an issue. I was learning firsthand the meaning of *cash-flow problem*.

One evening on my way home, I stopped at a Mexican restaurant I'd heard about. At the table next to mine were two women and a toddler, and because of the child's voluble friendliness, I ended up joining their conversation. The mother and her young daughter were visiting from Los Angeles, where the two women had once worked together.

"She's still working there," the woman from Honolulu said, "but I left the business and came here. I have an escort service right here in town."

Oh, *that* business. This attractive blonde had a bright I'm-taking-care-of-myself air, and when I mentioned that I was looking for work, she didn't miss a beat. "I'd hire you in a minute," she said.

I laughed. I told her that a few months before, I'd been a Hindu nun.

"Doesn't bother me," she said.

I was delighted by the contrast between where I had been and what had just been offered to me. "I got my first solid job offer," I told my boyfriend that night, "as a call girl."

Grady rolled his eyes. "This is your idea of solid?"

Well, not exactly, but hadn't the swami always talked about how God exists in every person and every place? Certainly, that must mean in every job as well! Not that I was going to get back to this woman, but her offer stayed in my mind. Her friend, the working mother from LA, did look flattened by her life, but the woman with her own business was radiant.

The next week, I visited the *Star-Bulletin*—I interviewed at both of the papers—and felt as if I were walking into a wax museum. So many people I knew were sitting at the same desks, doing the same work, looking exactly as they had when I'd left, eight years earlier. I asked one man on the copy desk, an old friend, what was happening in his life, and he said, "Just puttin' in my time, one paycheck to the next." He looked half-dead.

This, I thought, *is prostitution!* Of course, work brings financial compensation, but when you work only for the paycheck, you are selling yourself. You may be selling a different part of yourself than a sex worker does, and you may be selling that part for a different length of time, but what you're engaged in is, nonetheless, an act of whoring. I reflected that whatever work I ended up doing, I needed to do it for reasons connected to my heart.

This was a message I got from an old friend as well. Alvin Shim, a local labor lawyer, est graduate, and student of the swami, met me for lunch one day and asked what work I wanted to do. I started listing my professional skills: what I had done, what I could do . . .

"That was not the question," he said. "I'm not asking what you *can* do. What do you *want* to do?"

I didn't know what to say; my mind was blank.

"Okay," he said, "close your eyes. Ask yourself, *What would I do if I could do anything in the world?* See what comes up."

I saw it all; I could describe it to him in a flash: I wanted to live on my own, work at my own hours, and write for a living about subjects that interested me.

"Okay," Alvin said. "Now you know what you want to do. How do you get to that point from where you are now?" This is the big question.

◆ ◆ ◆

AS MY FIRST step, I accepted a part-time job handling finances and whatnot for a small, local publishing firm—now a one-and-a-half-person operation. It was the perfect place for me, taking me in the direction I wanted to go, something I would never have realized if I hadn't closed my eyes and answered Alvin's challenge. Not only was the atmosphere in this office congenial—the publisher kept his surfboard propped in a corner of the room—but the people who came and went were great leads for freelance writing and editing work.

I got the idea for my first magazine article from a young woman who had come to a workshop and a few chanting *satsangs* at the local ashram. I ran into her shopping, and the two of us went to lunch. She was interested in taking an English class at the University of Hawaii, she said, because there was something she wanted to write: "I want everyone to know that strippers are people, too."

This lovely young woman—with her bobbed hair and modest demeanor—was a professional striptease dancer and worked in one of Honolulu's biggest nightclubs. I never would have guessed.

"I can help you with this," I told her. "You take me around the clubs and introduce me to your friends, and I'll write the story for you. We'll do it together."

"The clubs" were dark and ugly, every one of them, but some of Monica's friends I will never forget. One, a sweet-faced twentysomething, had run away from a randy stepfather when she was in her midteens, before she had skills or schooling. Because she loved to dance, stripping seemed like a natural means of self-preservation. Her first set on stage that night was a delightful and energetic romp. As the record changed, she said, under her breath, "That was for me, and this one"—the new song came on, and she turned to face the lines of men, sitting in the dark with drinks before them—"is for you."

After the set, she said, "The guys who come here don't care about the dancing. I want to tell them, 'What more do you think you're going to see? I'm showing it *all* to you. There is nothing more to see!'"

Another of the strippers was approaching forty, like I was. She had a wiry body and an intelligent face; she was a handsome woman, not a pretty one. She said she had taken on stripping as spiritual challenge.

"Really? Tell me more about that."

"It's not easy to take your clothes off in front of a roomful of men," she said. "Most of these girls are high on something, and that's the only way they can do it. But a number of years ago in Arica, we—all of us pretty much middle-class girls—were challenged to get onstage in a strip club and take our clothes off. Some couldn't do it, and I found it really difficult. I decided I was going to take that on as a challenge, and I have spent years perfecting this. Now, I am completely comfortable taking my clothes off in front of men I don't know."

What bothered this woman was the question *So what?* "I'm almost forty," she said. "I won't be able to do this work much longer. I look at the time I gave to it, and I think, I could have done anything with those years. I could have studied medicine. I could be a doctor now. . . ."

I was moved by these women's stories, but by the time we had finished our nightclub rounds, I found that Monica and I were both a bit frustrated with our project. Each of us had gone into it with a secret agenda. I had felt that if Monica showed me her world, she might see it with fresh eyes and be inspired to find a more uplifting way to make a living. Monica, on the other hand, had felt that once I was comfortable with strippers, I might drop my inhibitions, step out onstage, and take off my own clothes. Neither of us got our wish.

◆ ◆ ◆

ANOTHER ARTICLE I researched and wrote at this time, one that was wholly satisfying, involved talking with five *kapuna*, Hawaiian elders, about the meaning of *aloha*. This ubiquitous word, spoken as a greeting and a farewell, actually means the love that's presumed to—and too often doesn't—give rise to those observances.

"Aloha is not something you do," said Pilahi Paki, a linguist whom the state of Hawaii considered a living treasure. "It's not even the way you do something. It is being in touch with yourself. When you are in that state, whatever you do expresses aloha."

She told me, "Say the word *aloha*."

I did: "Aloha."

"Now close your eyes and feel it. Take that word inside you and consider what it really means, consider the love inside you. Get in touch with that love, really feel it, and when you do feel it, then open your eyes and say that word again."

It was different the second time. I could feel the difference—there was a softness and a warmth—and I could hear the difference in my voice.

"Words are man's greatest weapon," Pilahi said, "and yet when people speak today, most of the time they have no sense of what they're saying. We have this idea that the faster someone speaks, the greater his intellect is, and so people use words frivolously, with no feeling of what they are saying."

Pilahi, a grandmother herself, said that in her own grandmother's day, for a Hawaiian to say the word *aloha* without a feeling of love in her heart was considered the same as lying.

Every one of the *kapuna* was a treasure, each in his own

way. It was an honor to meet them and an unmitigated delight to share their enlightened views in an article for *Aloha* magazine. Neither of these articles was, however, a boon to me financially. They both took longer to research and write than I'd thought they would—articles usually do—and when I finally received the checks, I saw that the fee I'd agreed to wouldn't go very far toward paying the rent and putting food on the table. I needed to find a more lucrative job. A *job* job!

I was also beginning to think it would be good to put a brake on the relationship I was in. My intuition told me that if I stayed where I was, we would end up marrying—and this wasn't what I needed in the moment.

◆ ◆ ◆

AT A BABY luau on Kailua Beach, I met the senior-most staff person for one of Hawaii's congressmen, back home between sessions. Hearing a bit of my story, he said that he might have something that would interest me. The congressman, he told me, had recently run into a tree and seen God. "He wants to write a book," the congressman's administrative assistant said. "You may be the right person to help him do that."

He was kidding about God but not, as it turned out, about either the tree or the book, which is why a few months later I moved to Washington, DC, to take a job as a congressional press aide. This congressman had indeed driven his car into a tree, and while lying in a hospital, recuperating from his accident, he'd read a newspaper article about brake defects in General Motors' A and J cars. He had been driving one of these and decided that he was the victim of defective brakes.

I was to write a book about this significant national issue, auto safety, on behalf of a congressman who had his own reasons for being interested. What he said was that his personal experience had brought his attention to a problem that was a grave danger to his constituents and to people everywhere. That is, of course, a possibility. Another view, held by some, is that beating the drum on brake defects gave the congressman

A congressional aide, in Washington, DC

added clout in the personal liability lawsuit he later brought against the car company. It was not a satisfying employment experience for me.

The first week I was on the job, my strippers article came out in *Honolulu* magazine, an unhappy surprise for the administrative assistant, whom I hadn't thought to mention it to. "Strippers vote," I told him. "They're constituents, too." But it was clear that, in my current position, I had more than just my own concerns at stake: I was representing a representative.

Then I had hello-nice-to-meet-you conversations with my new colleagues, one by one. To introduce myself, I talked about my background: leaving the press, going to India, having a teacher. "That's really interesting," several of them said, and everyone did seem interested—and open—while we talked. Afterward, however, the consensus was that I was . . . a little weird.

◆ ◆ ◆

THE SECOND SWAMI was at her ashram in the Northeast, her main facility in the United States and where she often spent the summer, giving lectures and workshops. The ashram was just a half-day's drive from Washington. As soon as I could, I took a long weekend to visit. I arrived halfway through the evening *satsang*. The hall was full, and I sat in the passageway just outside the open door. The second swami was speaking about the guru-disciple relationship. She said that the connection with a spiritual teacher is deep and internal, something that can be understood only by those who have experienced it.

Of course, she's right, I thought. *How could the people in my office possibly relate to my having a guru!*

In that moment, the swami started speaking about the nature of the guru, how the guru is more than just a teacher; the guru is one with the force that exists within every human being. I closed my eyes and realized that the swami's words were not coming in through my ears; her words were coming up through my body, as if they originated from deep inside me. As the words rose, they were illuminating layers of my own understanding.

I watched this inner event taking place, a part of my mind delighting in it while another part was thinking, *Is this really happening?* The swami stopped speaking then, and in the silence I moved my attention back to the swami herself, listening for what she would say next.

She said, "*This* is the guru-disciple relationship."

Whether the swami was referring to my focus on her in that moment or to the amazing play of her words inside me the moment before or to something else entirely—something she herself had just said—I knew I was engaged with my guru and was warmed by the thought.

◆ ◆ ◆

BACK IN WASHINGTON, I met two of the swami's other students who worked in offices on Capitol Hill, and we talked about the three of us perhaps giving an after-hours class on meditation. "I don't see how people survive in this place without meditating," one of them said, a young man who worked for the senator from his state and had been with the swami in India. I knew what he meant.

It wasn't a particularly high-energy period in my congressman's office—almost the entire nine months I was there, he was out of town, recuperating—and still this was a high-pressure place. The stacks of paper that formed as if by magic every day on my desk, the immediate deadlines, the need for accuracy, the feeling of being watched . . . It was like the newspaper, except that congressmen are elected every two years, which means there is no job security. Everyone in the congressman's office had an exit strategy—I suspect everyone on Capitol Hill does, at any given time. In a casual, all-office chat I learned that everyone but me wore a contraption to bed at night to keep from grinding their teeth while they slept. And who knows—perhaps if I'd stayed there longer, I would have been wearing one myself! Life was pulling at me.

Immediately after the swami's *samadhi*, I had found myself buoyed by unaccustomed energy, as if my departed teacher had given me a legacy. I felt as if I were floating above what had once been concerns in my life. People would say things I might have once found belittling or challenging or annoying, and no negative response would come up. I had preferences, but I was less invested in them than I once had been. It seemed as if I were coasting above my life in a glorious hot-air balloon, observing the play without being caught by it. I was content.

By the time two years had passed, however, I saw that my balloon had sprung leaks. I felt prodded by the dramas around me; once again they became *my* dramas. I felt challenged or upset by other people's insensitivity, their slowness to take in my perspective, their refusal to see that I was right. The contentment I'd thought of as mine had come, it turned out, from a fund of energy that I had been spending on mundane pursuits. Since I wasn't adding significantly to that store of energy through, say, daily meditation or chanting or contemplation, it was disappearing—and the vehicle of my consciousness was descending.

◆ ◆ ◆

ONE SIGN OF this change was that nine months on Capitol Hill was more than enough for me. It was time to leave this job—not only because I had almost finished the task for which I'd been hired but also because, in my last few days in Washington, I'd had a drink with a reporter from the newspaper chain I used to work for, spoken "off the record" about the congressman, and had her quote me by name in a splashy story that was highly unflattering to my employer. So the job was definitely over. All that was left was for me to drive cross-country, conducting the remaining interviews I had set up with brake-defect victims. From the West Coast, I would fly to Hawaii, where I would spend a month completing the manuscript. Though I knew by then that the book would never be published, I felt the need to finish the job I'd been hired to do.

As I made the contacts and set up the logistics for this trip, I thought about how doing PR work for a politician was considerably less satisfying than doing PR work for a saint. It didn't occur to me to return to the ashram, but I did decide that as long as I was going to write for a living, I should at least be writing from my own point of view. I got in touch with my old press contacts and, interspersed with interviews for the congressman's book, I set up job interviews for myself at a few newspapers across the country.

The first of the job interviews was in Knoxville, Tennessee. The editor told me he'd grown up poor there and wanted to give the city a good newspaper. I liked that. On my way out of town, I bought a pair of jeans and drove through the Great Smoky Mountains in a state of bliss as strong as anything I had experienced since the first swami's departure. The editor called me when I got to my parents' house—by then they had retired to Hot Springs, Arkansas—and we talked timing and money. Then I called him from a coffee shop in Albuquerque, and we shook hands over the phone.

When I got to Los Angeles, the second swami was there on a teaching tour, so I went to see her. At *darshan*, I told her,

"I'm going to be a reporter again." It had been ten years since I had met the swami as a newspaper reporter, and I thought she would laugh to hear I had come full circle. She did not laugh. She didn't even smile. She asked if I was a reporter—or a disciple.

"Uhh . . ." I paused to get my bearings. "What I had in mind was both," I said. I bowed again, physically if not in spirit, and made a fast exit. It was the wrong answer.

That night I considered what I had gained from my time serving the swami: the opening of my heart, the clearing out of my mind, the straightening up of my health, my ability to take care of myself in this world—all of it had come through my association with the guru. Here I was, driving alone on a cross-country trip I had arranged for and managed all on my own, doing interviews to accomplish this unsatisfying job with a gracious gesture of completion, meeting new people at every turn, making definitive decisions about the next step in my life. Where had the moxie come from to handle all of this? Yet where was it I turned when my job was a disappointment? To journalism? Why hadn't I even considered yoga?

The next day when I saw the second swami, I told her I wanted to come back to the ashram—but that I'd made a commitment.

Go to Knoxville, I was told. Work for a year. Save money.

It was that last part that gave me a problem.

◆ ◆ ◆

I WAS ON my way to Knoxville, driving across the Mojave Desert, when it occurred to me I was afraid of the ashram. I had been so extreme there. I was living in a balanced way now, and I cherished that. I didn't want to give it up. When I arrived in Knoxville, I did a lot of things. I threw myself into my job. I wrote about Knoxville's first gay pride celebration, and—like a take from *Doonesbury*—I wrote about living in homeless shelters, visiting miners who had black lung, and even committing myself to the state mental facility (for a long weekend). I did interesting interviews, made some great friends, hiked in the Smoky Mountains, adopted two cats from a Kroger parking lot, attended a storytelling festival in Jonesboro, framed artwork and potted plants for my apartment, added to my wardrobe, learned how to make bread and beer . . . I did a lot of things that might be construed as "having a life."

What I didn't do was save money.

I didn't even remember I was supposed to save money or that the second swami had given me a year to be in Knoxville.

After I'd been there about eleven months, there was a shift in the management policy at the newspaper, and it was clear that the editor's journalistic ideals weren't nearly as important to him as profits. The efforts of a young, hardworking, enthusiastic staff were cashed in for the sole benefit of a strong bottom line. I wanted out; I wanted to offer my energy to help put light into the universe; I wanted to go back to the ashram.

On my vacation, I arranged to visit the East Coast ashram, where the second swami was once again in residence. On the drive there, it occurred to me that I was going to be seeing the swami precisely one calendar year after our last meeting. It was then that I remembered: I was supposed to go to Knoxville for a year—*and I was supposed to save money!* I hadn't. I had no savings. I hadn't even brought an offering for the guru, a colossal oversight in light of Indian tradition. Before I got to the ashram, I stopped at a store and bought a tiny silver box in the shape of a heart. It was a trinket, but at least I had something.

The next day I sat on a shady stretch of lawn with some other people, each of us waiting to be called to speak with the second swami. She was sitting in a small chair under gigantic oaks that stood behind an outdoor pavilion, and beside her was the largest dog I had ever seen: a Great Dane about the size of a small pony. I kept eyeing the dog, uneasy about going anywhere near a carnivore of that size. The dog was sitting on the ground, next to second swami's chair, and his head was as high as hers. Just before I walked up to her, she sent the dog away. Then I had only the guru to face.

"Having a life," in Knoxville

I presented her with my gift; she made the observation that it was a heart, and she paused. She asked me what was in it.

I knew what she meant. I told her, "I want to come back to the ashram. I really know that I want to be here now. But I didn't save any money."

Go to Knoxville, she said. Work for a year. Save money.

It was, word for word, what she'd said a year earlier. I hadn't remembered the second swami's instruction to me, but she had. This time I followed it.

By taking on some freelance assignments and introducing some small austerities to my life—packing my lunches, shopping at thrift stores, curtailing any expensive entertainments—in the space of about nine months, I was able to put aside what was, for a member of the working press, a substantial chunk of money. Still, it didn't feel like enough to consider going for a length of time with no paycheck. It was a fraction of what

I'd received in my divorce, the property settlement that had funded my following the swami years before.

I sent the second swami a letter, telling her that I felt I needed to work and save a bit longer before returning to the ashram. I heard back that, of course, this would be fine, and I started looking for a job on a bigger, better-paying newspaper.

I had arranged for an interview at a paper in Maryland that was known to be a "feeder" to the *Washington Post*, one of my favorite publications. I was planning to visit the East Coast ashram at the end of the summer, and I set up the interview for the week before. As I was solidifying my plans, someone in the ashram said that the week I was planning to be there, no public *satsangs* would be held. "If you want to see the swami," she said, "you should think about coming a week earlier."

I considered this for about two minutes before calling the newspaper and moving the interview up by a week. I'd do it on the way back from the ashram, not on the way there.

◆ ◆ ◆

THE WEEK BEFORE I left, I made an impromptu visit to an old boyfriend who had recently moved to a new job in Nashville. This had not been a serious relationship for either of us, but I felt like being with someone that weekend, and so I went to see him, saying I wanted to see his new apartment and taking him a housewarming gift.

That night we went to a movie he was eager to see: *Alien II*. "It'll be exciting," he said. Electrifying is what it was. I hadn't seen the first *Alien* movie, so I had no idea what I was in for. I felt queasy for days afterward, as if I were sick someplace deeper than my stomach.

On my long drive to the ashram that next week, I contemplated why two hours of fantasy horror would have such a compelling impact on my state of mind. It came to me that I saw the film as a symbol of the current state of my *sadhana*, my journey to self-knowledge. Here I was, engaging with life, playing out various dramas, indulging my desires . . . All of these mental impressions were going inside me, just like that movie had, and at some point a few of these impressions—we could call them karmas, for that's what I saw them as—would erupt from me, fully fledged, as monsters, my monsters.

It occurred to me that I hadn't been thinking about the second swami for the past few months, and as I considered this, the reason came to me: I was furious with her. Here I had worked so hard to save money, and she'd said it wasn't enough!

No. The second swami had never said that. She had just reflected back to me what I'd written to her. I was the one who'd said I didn't have enough money. Suddenly, I knew that this was the auspicious time for my return to the swami's world. It could happen right now. I could be back in India in a month's time.

I arrived at the ashram in a state of exhilaration.

When I went up for *darshan*, the second swami gave me an impassive glance and asked how long I'd be staying this time.

"Let's make it long-term," I said. "I'd like to come with you to India right now, on this trip."

The second swami continued to bless people who came before her, looking at each of them as she did, and it seemed as if her attention wasn't even on me when she sent me to speak to one of her secretaries. As I turned to go, she called after me that I could come—but I'd have to sit at the back of the plane.

I felt triumphant. I sat against the wall, weeping, laughing. I knew that those words were prophetic. I would be sitting at the back of the plane in every respect. In that moment, I didn't care. I was thrilled to go along for the ride.

21. ❧ This May Look Like an Ordinary Place

WHEN WE ARRIVED IN INDIA a month later, though the ashram looked much the same, the ashram culture had changed perceptibly since I had last lived full-time with the swami. Ashramites now dressed with more polish. They played larger roles in the organization, and the organization itself was more substantial. Balaram, who had cooked for a year in the little ashram in Hawaii, was now in charge of all ashram construction, with hundreds of skilled carpenters and other tradesmen working under him. The crowds that came were bigger, the classes better organized, the publications more refined. The fundamentals remained unchanged, but in many ways I found it to be a new world. I had no position in this world, no role to play, and I found this especially challenging. I was, as the swami had warned, sitting at the back.

As I entered the ashram's chai shop, I saw two people I felt I knew fairly well—another former *brahmacharya* and a man I'd had many conversations with in the past and who had brought me a little gift the last time I'd seen him in India, some ten years before. These two were sitting by themselves at a long table. Good, someone I could talk with. I went to buy chai, and by the time I'd returned, several people I didn't know had sat down at the table. I joined them anyway, sitting several seats away from my friends and experiencing a frisson of acute discomfort in the hesitant hellos and introductions. I had presumed to join a group to which I didn't have admittance: all these people, including my two old friends, played significant roles in the guru's world, and I no longer did.

In this instance, I was saved. Someone came running up and said that the swami, who was giving *darshan* in the courtyard, was asking for me—she had a perfect *seva* for me.

This may have been the swami's direct and conscious intervention, or it may have been coincidence; from my perspective, it was perfect timing. I gulped down my chai and rushed to the courtyard to hear what task the swami had in mind for me.

I was to give orientations for newly arrived Westerners. This was a side *seva*, something I would do in addition to other tasks, something that expanded and contracted with the ashram head count. Over certain holidays, visitors would throng to the ashram, and the orientation sessions were then held several times a day for twenty, thirty, fifty people. We sat in the gardens, on the marble steps of the small open pavilion, the *mandap*, of the goddess Durga. As befits a goddess, the statue was about twice the height of most women, dressed in a gold-trimmed silk sari, holding the ritually correct weapon in each of her six outstretched hands, and sitting upon a snarling tiger. Under Durga's beneficent gaze, I'd talk about the daily schedule, domestic necessities like laundry and meals, and one other issue I always found a way to bring up.

"This may look like an ordinary place," I'd say—though, come to think of it, with a giant goddess looking over my shoulder, just how *ordinary* could it possibly have appeared to these people? But the warning always seemed important: "The ashram isn't at all ordinary," I'd tell them. "You have just stepped into a cauldron of energy . . . ," and then I'd find some way to talk about how they were likely to find they had reactions to anything, to everything—reactions that were exponentially more intense than usual. They might experience inexplicable joy

In India, 1988

upon hearing a wind chime; they might want to slap someone who cut in front of them in a line.

This is the nature of a holy place, I'd explain. In this divine atmosphere, in this energy, you have the opportunity to see and hear what's in the recesses of your mind, what's been hidden there all along. And if you are able to witness these reactions—if, as you have these reactions, you continue to repeat your mantra or chop vegetables or chant a traditional text—the power of your practice can steady the ecstasy and lift you out of the rage so this garbage you've been carrying within you begins to dissipate, to disappear.

It was prudent advice. Sometimes I was able to follow it myself. On this visit, at the very time when I was giving these orientations, I found myself unable—or unwilling—to do so and was embroiled in any number of my unworthy responses.

◆ ◆ ◆

I HAD A reaction to sitting at the back. It was more difficult for me than I had ever imagined it could be. I'd never understood just how much prestige I'd had in my life—as a journalist, an ashram manager, a congressional aide. Now I was nobody special.

I became focused on the beautiful jewelry, especially the rings, that the women around me all seemed to be wearing and that many of them seemed to have received as gifts from the swami. Years before, I'd looked at the heavens and said, "I. Want. That. Ring." Then, the ring symbolized assuming a role, being in a marriage, joining with another person. This wasn't so very different. The ring still represented a role, still showed someone's acceptance of me. Everything I wanted in life was suddenly contained in a piece of jewelry.

It sounds idiotic. It *was* idiotic, as well as shallow, grasping, childish—a raft of qualities I didn't like to think I had. But I wanted a ring!

The swami herself had given me a teaching on the subject of desire when I'd seen her two years before, in Los Angeles. That evening in *darshan* she had given me a small, enameled box. It was lovely, painted gold, with a lattice-like design of flowering branches, and in the branches was an exquisite little bird. I was enormously happy to receive this gift, and in her talk that night, the swami seemed to be commenting on my response.

We're so delighted to receive something from the guru, she said, but what is it, after all? It's only a box. Will that box take you across this world? Will you attain anything by its presence in your life? Will it satisfy you? There it will be, years from now, sitting on your bedside table . . .

That night, I went back to my upper bunk in an ashram dorm room, thinking about the swami's talk. As if to prove her wrong, I picked up the tiny wooden box with both hands, like it was the Holy Grail—it had, after all, been touched by my guru—and held it to my heart. I was shocked at the intensity of the love I could feel radiating from it. *Only* a box? I sat holding this box to my heart for fully an hour, feeling that the swami's own energy was coming through it, piercing my heart with a love that then poured through my whole body, filled me, and radiated from me.

The experience didn't do much to break my attachment to receiving gifts from the guru. And that, I think, is what the swami wanted to teach me. It's certainly something I needed to learn.

As the swami had said it would, that box now sat on my bedside table, largely ignored. What could a ring possibly do for me?

Still, a ring was what I wanted: a ring from the second swami.

I knew I should apply yogic principles here, but I didn't even consider the swami's suggestion of rising above my desire. Instead, I chose another teaching, one more to my liking. I knew that the guru isn't just the person of swami; the guru is a cosmic force of grace, and in that sense, each one of us carries the capacity to be the guru. So I gave myself a ring.

I found a nice ring at a price I could afford, and I was quite happy with it. It had a cluster of tiny rubies; I liked their color and sparkle and the way the ring gave a look of distinction to my hand. I didn't pretend the swami had given me the ring; I told my little story of desire and fruition with satisfaction, feeling as if I had come to some understanding. It wasn't a permanent fix.

◆ ◆ ◆

IN THE MEANTIME, I had also become embroiled in an infatuation—*another* infatuation. It was a surprise—a shock, in fact—to discover that I was once again vulnerable in this way. In my four years of working, I'd lived in three different cities and had had a boyfriend in each city. One of them I'd lived with for six months. I was not infatuated with these men. I liked each of them, was fond of them, found each attractive, but I was not in any way *absorbed* in them. Also, I had come back to the ashram to support the second swami; I wasn't there to find a man.

The issue came up shortly after my arrival. During the first few days, while walking through the courtyard, I heard an inner voice say, *The next thing in your* sadhana *will be to have a child.*

Great! There I was, forty-one and living in an ashram in India with no prospects for a mate even remotely in view!

The inner voice added, *And* he *is going to be the avenue through which it will happen.* In that moment my head swiveled, as if by some invisible force, ninety degrees to the left, so that my eyes rested on a particular man, someone who had been extremely friendly to me over chai just the day before.

Unfortunately (actually, fortunately), this man's own inner voice did not speak to him on the same matter, or, if it did, what it said was something considerably different. When I thought about it later, I saw that if I hadn't received that subtle message, I never would have opened up to this man—and with desire, it's the opening up, it's those first steps forward, that set the drama in motion. When I began showing interest, he began backing off. I thought I must be mishandling a relationship that was supposed to happen. I was supposed to be with this man, right? He was the one with whom I was to have this child that had been asked of me, right? I began to focus on him, look for him, ponder what I was doing wrong.

And before very long, I was once again caught in an infatuation.

It's not that I had learned nothing from my first experience. I didn't make the same kinds of mistakes I'd made with Terrence. I didn't tell anyone about that initial inner message. And I didn't wait very long before I brought up the issue with the swami.

I was standing in line for *darshan* one morning, intending to lay it before her that day, when I had a thought: *You should offer the swami your ring.* I brushed this idea aside with annoyance. The swami had no need for a ring. She would never wear it herself. She would give it to someone else, one of those people to whom she gave jewelry.

When I got to the head of the line, I bowed and asked the swami if I could talk with her about something that was troubling me. A meeting was arranged for later that day or the next. There was enough time to buy another ruby ring to give the swami—my solution to that inner request: this way I could have my ring and she'd have hers.

The swami saw me in a small, shady marble courtyard near

her living quarters. I told her about what had been happening with this particular man.

He's too young for you, she told me. That was true. He was two or three years younger in physical years, and we were exceedingly different in other respects. That was part of what had attracted me: I saw him as a diamond in the rough.

I told her then about the directive I'd received from that inner voice about having a child, and she said that this meant I was going to have a spiritual rebirth.

This is one of the reasons a person has a spiritual guide. I would never have divined that meaning on my own, and, given the interpretation, I could see that my humbling experience with yet another infatuation had opened me up in a way that I'd needed. It was, indeed, an avenue to rebirth.

I gave the swami the ruby ring I had gotten for her and told her the rest of the story: how I had wanted a ring from the guru and had given myself one, knowing that I, too, was the guru. I'd decided to keep that ring, I told her, and give her another ruby ring. As I was going through this explanation, what I was feeling inside was *wrong, wrong, wrong!*

The swami told me that she had brought something for me as well. She dropped a beautiful garnet pendant into my hand. It looked a lot like a ruby, but it wasn't, and I knew this was significant. All gemstones have their own properties, and the special power of the garnet, I later read, is to raise one's energy to a higher frequency—remedial assistance I was clearly in need of. And the ruby? The ruby is associated with love and passion, among other qualities. It occurred to me that when a spiritual master gives a gift, it is not a token of affection; it's medicinal on a subtle level. It's for the recipient's spiritual benefit.

◆ ◆ ◆

THE SWAMI WAS about to go on a teaching tour to Delhi. On the day before she left, there was a concert of classical Indian music in the large courtyard. A crowd had gathered; I sat at the back with my eyes closed. As I listened to the sweet tones of the *vina*, I remembered the time in the Indian hospital when I'd awakened in a state of unconditional love. As I recalled the experience of this profound and all-encompassing ecstasy, an inner voice cut into my reverie:

You don't need me.

Within me, everything stopped. There was no courtyard, no music, no memory of glory. I felt certain this was the second swami speaking to me, and so I addressed her, also speaking in my mind: *What do you mean, I don't need you? You know how unbaked I am.*

You don't need me, the voice repeated, shifting the emphasis. *You've known God, and the swami will come for you when you die. He'll take you across. Why would you need me?*

I felt chilled. This conversation was real—it was happening on a subtle level, but it was truly happening—and it felt like the most important exchange of my life. *That's not enough*, I thought. *I don't want to have known God once and then go to him again at the end of my life. I want to live in that experience. I want it to be a reality for me, minute by minute.*

The response came: *For that you'll have to give up everything.*

I felt as if I were being told I had to give up the guarantee that the swami would take me across. *I'll do that*, I thought. *I trust you.*

Then give me the ring!

The ring? I had forgotten all about the ring! In this moment, the concert ended; *darshan* began almost as I was opening my eyes. Before I could move, the line in front of the swami's chair became both long and wide, and it seemed it would be hours before I could get to the front of it. I thought, *I'll do this later* and started to walk away. As I got to the courtyard steps, a man took the microphone and said, "The swami asked me to tell you"—I stopped in my tracks—"that two of the deer in the upper garden had a fight today, and one of them lost his antler. He had the antler offered to the swami. She wanted me to tell you, 'Even an animal knows to give *dakshina.*'"

Dakshina is a material offering to the guru. Whether the offering is large or small, whether it is something precious or something as modest as the ring I was pulling from my finger as I leaped into the *darshan* line, the traditional view—and my view—is that this offering by the disciple is insignificant compared with the inner gifts given him by the guru. It's also understood that the very act of offering opens the disciple to receive.

It didn't take long to get to the front of the line, but once I was there, bowing before the swami, it seemed an impossible matter to give her the ring. In India, the ashram's *darshan* lines were complex. Banked in front of the guru's chair were several sets of *padukas*, the guru's shoes, arrayed on short pedestals. If you wished to speak with the guru, or hand her something, as I was attempting to do, you had to be in one of the special lines on either side. I hadn't planned this properly, and I was directly in the center, behind the *padukas* and a couple of yards from the guru's chair. As I sat there, studying the situation, I saw a woman to the far left give the swami a ring to bless; the swami took this ring for a moment and handed it back to the woman. How was I going to get my ring to the swami? And how was I going to let her know what this was about? She might not understand.

At that moment, the swami looked at me. It was a look of utter focus, and she wasn't smiling. She reached over to a side table, picked something up, and thrust it at me across the *padukas*. Only then did I see what it was—she was pointing to me with the antler. I slipped the ring on the tip of the antler, and the swami deposited it on her table with a little clink: the guru taking what was hers. What she wanted wasn't the ring; she wanted my unholy attachment to it.

I laughed and bowed again, this time alight with joy. Letting go of that ring felt so much more satisfying than having it ever did.

I got the feeling of connection I'd wanted. It had been up to me all along.

EPILOGUE ᕐ *The Great Forest*

THAT'S A LONG VERSION OF MY STORY. Here is a short one: At twenty-one, with a new journalism degree and a hundred dollars in my pocket, I flew to Hawaii to be in a former roommate's wedding. My plan was to start a new life, as far as possible from Evanston, Illinois, where I'd gone to school, and Tulsa, Oklahoma, where I'd spent my formative years. In Hawaii I joined the working press, embarked on romantic adventures, learned to snorkel, drank wine on the beach, married, bought a cottage, gardened, took in a cat . . . After eight years, even though my life seemed to be exactly what I'd set out to find, I came to the understanding that it wasn't working. Why?

The answer is best conveyed, I think, by another story from the *Yoga Vasishtha*, "The Great Forest." A celestial being, walking in a vast wooded expanse, encounters a restless creature with a thousand arms and legs. Though there is no one else around, the creature is clearly frightened. He's armed with a mace, and he's hitting himself with it. The creature bellows and weeps and runs to hide—from himself!

Seeing this endless cycle of pain, the celestial takes compassion on the creature. With the strength of his will, he restrains the creature long enough to ask, "Who are you?" At this, the creature becomes frantic with terror. He turns his abuse on the celestial, calls him vile names, sneers at him. Left on his own again, the creature continues his self-immolation.

Occasionally in this forest, the celestial encounters a self-destructive creature who responds to the question and contemplates his own bleak condition. Such a one, the scripture says, can find freedom.

As with all parables, everything in the story is a symbol: the forest is the circumstance of our lives, and the creature is our own mind, the nervous trickster that creates enmity and strife for us where none needs exist. That's what my mind was doing to me.

I, by age twenty-nine, had come to understand that I was a primary cause of my own discontent. So, when I did an interview for the newspaper with a visiting master of meditation, I was ready to hear his wisdom, put down my mace, and follow him. That journey, which became the new circumstance of my life, lasted for about thirty-five years. Except for one four-year hiatus, I spent that time living in ashrams. To still my mind, I meditated, chanted God's name, read sacred texts, but I also edited a monthly magazine and later a website; I worked on course scripts and the sorts of written communications a nonprofit sends its supporters.

Then, at age sixty-three, I embarked on another journey. I left my teacher's ashram and went to an island—not Hawaii this time but another island, in the Pacific Northwest—to begin yet another new life.

◆ ◆ ◆

MY DEPARTURE FROM the ashram on the U.S. East Coast was as much a pilgrimage as following the swami had been. Once again, the most crucial step was realizing I would embark on a journey at all. This time, it was a matter of listening. Leaving the ashram wasn't a new topic for me. Over the years I'd had hundreds of conversations about leaving the ashram—about the possibility that I might leave and the fact that various other people *were* leaving.

As I've indicated, an ashram is a place of refuge, a place of spiritual practice and study, a place of service, but generally it isn't a place where anyone other than a monk spends the rest of her life. At one point or another, most of my colleagues and closest friends had left the ashram to start new careers, care for parents, raise children, explore the arts, and so on. I saw them off with gifts and kisses and well wishes, and in some cases I kept in touch, but my basic attitude was *there but for the grace of God* . . . I thought if I could be strong enough, I'd be able to stay.

One day before the noon chant, I heard something else. The second swami came to the chant and, walking to her seat, paused to question a four-year-old boy. The child's best friend, a six-year-old, had recently left with her parents to return home to France. Did the boy miss his friend? Had he written to her? Oh, so he had *called* her. Was it fun to talk with her on the phone? Was this like being with her?

In the back-and-forth, I observed that the swami was speaking about people who had just left the ashram. Then I heard, as a thought, *It's time for you to go.*

This message was as clear as any oral or written instruction I have ever received. The inner direction may have come before, but this was the first time I heard it. If I hadn't heard it on that day, I'm certain it would have come again, and again—each time more strongly, until, finally, the message would have been given in such a way that I *had* to hear it.

In my observation, it's easier to follow instructions that come from inside me than to follow those delivered aloud by virtually anyone else. It's as if, for me, spoken words are a kind of bludgeon. I don't know why that is. It isn't that I thought I had any real choice about this inner message. I saw *it's time for you to go* not as an invitation but as a command, a call to action.

At the same time, that's all it was. With years of practice in meditation—practice in watching my own mind—I was able to take in this instruction without the emotional freight I might once have attached to it. *It's time for you to go* didn't mean I had failed or was less worthy than those who were staying; it didn't raise in me a fear about what would happen next or flood me with questions about what I would do to support myself. And *it's time for you to go* didn't mean *in this very minute*!

Actually, that I was able to hear this instruction as I did, coming from inside, may have meant that I had a more gracious length of time to plan my journey. That afternoon I spoke to my supervisor in the area where I offered *seva*, and the next morning, I called the ashram's human resources department. It was, however, fully a year before I drove away from the ashram in my capriciously overstuffed car. By then I'd had plenty of time to prepare—to decide, for instance, where I might go. For that I had to do a bit of looking.

◆ ◆ ◆

MANY OF MY friends who've made a big move in their sixties have done so in order to be with family: parents, children, grandchildren. There was never a question where these people would go, but this wasn't true for me. My parents had died; I had no children; I was fond of my only brother but not close to him. For years I'd thought of the ashram as home, and what I needed now was a new home. I needed to be able to support myself as well, but I had professional skills. Finding a place to live was my main task. What should I look for?

As I considered what was most important for me, I saw I wasn't going to become someone else on this journey. What had mattered to me for the last thirty-five years was still going to matter: I needed a place where I'd be supported in my meditation. That meant the place should be beautiful but not so beautiful that hordes of people live there. It should be quiet but close to culture and not so small it's provincial. And the local people should be friendly to others who aren't exactly like them—to those, say, who've lived for three decades in an ashram. They should be willing to think of such people as family.

In two trips, I looked at four places. By *looking* I mean that

On an exploratory trip, 2007

I stayed with friends, did some work, negotiated highways, went for walks, ate out, visited meditation centers, and asked everyone I met how they felt about living there. Actually, I looked *and* listened. When I told a young man behind an airport coffee counter I was thinking about moving to that city, he said, "Why would you want to do that?" He meant it.

In the last place I went—Whidbey Island in Washington State—I was planning only to see a friend. I hadn't seriously considered Whidbey. This forested island is idyllic but too small, too rural; I'd never be able to support myself in a place like Whidbey. And yet, ultimately, that was where I wanted to live. What clinched it was when my friend, a retired professor, told me, "If I were moving to a city today, I have no idea how I'd make new friends. On Whidbey you see someone at the post office, you see them at the market, you talk to them at a meeting—and suddenly you know that person. It's organic." That's what I was looking for: organic.

That something is organic does not mean that it's automatic or even especially easy. My trip cross-country had its challenges. Life on the road requires a precision with objects that I, a wordsmith, had never developed. I found that, to adapt a phrase, stuff happened. *Stuff* like losing my car keys in Ohio, dropping a credit card at a Starbucks in Minnesota, leaving my purse (with all my identification and money) on a picnic table in the badlands of North Dakota. With each mishap, my stomach would clench—and then, as one must, I did what was needed. Courtesy of AAA, I got the car towed to a dealer who could make new keys; I canceled the missing credit card and was glad I carried another; and the badlands didn't turn out to be so bad after all. A woman who noticed me looking for my purse told me, "The park ranger has it; I turned it in at the office."

After I'd been on Whidbey Island a couple of months, I fell and broke my arm, which, because I was living alone, I found to be a particular trial. About this time, I had a dream in which I was looking for a button to push. I needed to push a certain button, and I simply *had* to find this button. As I was coming out of sleep, I realized that I was looking for the button that would make everything all right. I woke up laughing— because, of course, there is no such button.

There was never a guarantee that my adventure in the great forest would turn out "all right"—meaning, the way I wanted it to. But I've noticed that every time something goes "wrong," I have an opportunity to become more conscious and—just as significant—to have a new kind of interaction with the people around me, sometimes with total strangers. When I broke my arm, members of the meditation group on Whidbey, several of whom I had just met, brought me meals; others went with me to my medical appointments. "This is what friends do," one woman said, and she's had occasion to say this several times since, because over the last few years she's been an enormous help to me. I hope, from time to time, I have been for her as well.

My most significant strategy on this journey of discovery has been to reach out. To this end, I took a part-time job in the local library, joined a community choir, moved to a village where I can walk to many of the things I like doing, and adopted a gregarious dog who takes me out for daily walks. These are choices I didn't know to make in my twenties, when I moved to that other island. This time I am finding what's right for me.

There are other joys as well. I arrived on Whidbey during blackberry season, the time between August and the autumn rains when erupting from every culvert, cranny, and vacant lot are juicy, sweet berries, half the size of my thumb and warm from the sun. I began to scatter blackberries over ice cream, through cereal, and across grilled salmon; to bake them into cobblers, pies, and muffins; and to share these treats with neighbors and droppers-by and friends who asked me over. Feeding oneself and one's friends is commonplace, perhaps, but it's an exquisite pleasure for an anorectic who could have lost her life from fear of food.

And that other bête noire of mine, infatuation, hasn't had a toehold. Or perhaps it's the opposite: now I'm infatuated with just about everyone. It's astonishing to me how much beauty there is in the people I meet. There's the shy man who comes every day to feed a small tribe of feral cats on the bluff at the end of the block. There's the eighty-eight-year-old woman who lives down the street, making elaborate beaded handbags to hang on the walls of her immaculate apartment. I had breakfast with her one morning and was agog at her meticulously kept collections: antique clocks and books, vintage shoes and hats with netting.

I talked with a local artist about her paintings: a huge, happy orangutan, reaching out as if to touch someone (but gently); a herd of blocky horses, facing in many directions as if responding to different cues (but with clarity); and a window with rays of light coming through it. Nothing else: just the window and the light. That was the one that most interested me, both the image itself and what the artist had to say about it. The painting was inspired by a story she'd read as a child and had never forgotten but never again found, a story about a little girl who almost lost the light from her life because she didn't know that in order to experience light, you need to keep your attention on it.

That is what I do now in my life, what I learned to do in my years of living in an ashram: the effort, if you want to call it that, is to bring my attention back to whatever is coming up for me in any moment. That's my light. It's what I am. It's what I have, and it is more than enough.

Author's Note

IN ALL, I SPENT THIRTY YEARS LIVING IN ASHRAMS. To span this experience in a book, I had to make some huge leaps in time. The incidents themselves are as accurate as my memory and auxiliary resources will support. Most—not all— of the names have been changed, but the people themselves are as I remember them.

My reasons for not identifying my spiritual path or the names of my teachers are straightforward. I am a student and do not want my experiences and recollections to be taken as teachings of the path. Besides, I would never want to imply that I think mine is the only valid path. Clearly, it isn't. It is my path; it may or may not be yours.

There are, however, universal truths in spiritual endeavor, recognized on every path. For instance, if I were to write a beginners' guide to meditation now, I would keep it to three instructions: *breathe; love; be with one who meditates*—understanding that this is someone who's in a state of meditation all the time. That's the heart of it, I feel, and, as simple as it sounds, I think it's enough.

When I began writing this book, the first vignette I put into words was also my favorite. It offered a glimpse into ashram life. It gave the seminal teaching of the book. It indicated how someone can learn from moment-by-moment events—and, by inference, from a book such as this.

Finally, I had to admit that this unparalleled vignette did not fit with the rest of my story. What to do?

It stands on its own, the afterword.

AFTERWORD ☙ *Kristina*

IT WAS EARLY AFTERNOON ON A SUNNY DAY at the summer's end. The second swami had just completed a public program for several thousand of her students in the main hall of the ashram in the northeastern United States. She had stopped by the elevator at the end of the lobby to say goodbye to two people leaving for home, when the ashram's current dog, a golden retriever named Mackenzie, appeared.

Earlier, the swami had mentioned that among all of the auspicious signs for this particular day—it was Labor Day; the final day of a summer workshop; the fiftieth lunar anniversary of the first swami's *divya diksha*, his spiritual initiation—it was also Mackenzie's birthday! So the crowd in the lobby took the opportunity to sing "Happy Birthday" to Mackenzie as he loped around the lobby, barking.

Mackenzie's enthusiasm seemed to draw the swami back into the lobby and out the front door, where she sat down in the shade of the portico. The breeze ruffled the wind chimes overhead, and the swami chatted with those who were there, greeting, teasing, and, as I suspect she does in every minute of her day, taking care of people.

At one point, she spotted a ninety-year-old woman standing by a pillar in the middle of what were by now a hundred onlookers and asked someone to bring the woman a chair. When a man came forward who had problems with his knees, the swami asked for a chair for him as well. It was with the children, however, that this loving alertness was most apparent.

As with any family gathering on any front porch, attention went to the youngest members of the group. At first it was a one-year-old who was exploring, fingerprinting, drooling onto, and finally climbing a six-inch-high Plexiglas encasement for the *rangoli*, the festive designs in chalk that welcome people at the ashram entrance. The swami had just one comment to the girl's mother: her daughter was well coordinated.

Only when an older and larger child, a boy of three, started to join the toddler on the plastic case was a restriction introduced. The boy wasn't told no; he was coaxed to play elsewhere. And it wasn't because he posed a danger to the plastic; it was that the plastic was a danger for him. The swami observed that everything in a public place of this sort needed to be childproof. Parents were right here and watching, she said, so no problems would come up now. But parents can't always watch, and at another time someone could get hurt.

This wasn't an idle observation. There were people on the sidelines taking note of the swami's counsel. The next day there would be meetings, discussions, plans, a proposal, a requisition, perhaps a work crew. People would ask themselves why they hadn't seen this problem when they walked through the area. It was a tiny, precise, perfectly aimed lesson in being conscious.

As this play unfolded, there sat on the far side of the *rangoli* a girl of about three who made no move to join the other two children. You must be shy, the swami said to her, and with that the girl began speaking . . . about her mama, about her dad, about the first swami. "*My* swami," she said. "My swami lives at home." When she was asked where her home was, she pointed at her mother.

Much that she said, however, wasn't quite so easy to follow, and it delighted me to watch the second swami drawing the child out, asking her question after question, trying to follow what she was saying. Oh, so he's *your* swami. Where is he? He's on the beach? He walks on the beach? Does he walk *only* on the beach? Yes, we know that's your mama. We've got that now. Where is your papa? Oh, so your name is Kristina. And on and on, with absolute patience, the swami talked with this little girl.

Then she asked David to step forward. David is, among other things, a juggler and sleight-of-hand master and always happy to entertain. He began to throw objects into the air and keep them aloft, ending with a showy piece that involved all of the candles around the *rangoli*. The crowd was laughing and applauding because not only is David adept, he also is enormously amusing with his pretense of blundering and bungling, of being always an inch from catastrophe, while never dropping a thing.

Little Kristina was asked if she enjoyed the show, and she shook her head. When pressed, she said, "No."

There was a lot of laughter about this and also some surprise, until the swami made an observation: David took over the stage, didn't he? The swami then called forward Allegra, who, she explained, tells beautiful stories.

Allegra told a story especially for and especially *to* Kristina, so it seemed the little girl herself was onstage, truly a part of the tale. It was a brilliant recast of "The Goose That Laid the Golden Eggs" . . . and in the end, the king let the goose go free, back to the forest, and the next day the goose produced a beautiful, shining golden egg, the largest and most valuable that had ever been seen in the world, and carried it back in the crook of her wing to present to the king.

As Allegra neared the end of her story, Kristina turned her back and began to talk to her mother.

What did he name it? the swami asked.

"And what do you think the king named the egg?" Allegra asked, addressing Kristina's back. "What do you think? He named it . . ." She paused, and the entire assemblage, by now about 150 people, called out in unison, "*Kristina*."

Kristina smiled.

"Did you like Allegra's story?" the swami asked her.

Silence. Kristina didn't actually shake her head no, but she didn't nod, either, and she certainly never said yes.

A singer stood up then and said, "There's nothing like a

song." She forged an instant adaptation of a favorite from *West Side Story*: "Kris-teen-AHHH. I've just met a girl named Kris-teen-ahhh. . . ." The crowd picked it up, and scores of people began serenading this delighted little girl. *Kris-teen-AHHH!* She loved it. She looked around at the circle of loving faces and smiled in what seemed to be awestruck wonder. People had fathomed the kind of attention she wanted, and they were willing to give it to her.

When the swami rose to go inside, Kristina was reluctant for this delicious exchange to end. "I don't want to go home," she said.

The swami told Kristina that she could go to the ashram temple and see the *murti*, the statue, of her guru's guru, who would please the child the way no juggler or storyteller in the world could ever do. From the inside, the swami said; he'll please you from the inside.

◆ ◆ ◆

THIS TABLEAU WAS tiny and, to my mind, also epic. In years to come, Kristina may not remember much of it, but I imagine she'll hear about her exchange with the swami so many times from her family, she'll feel as if she does remember it. If she allows herself to take the story in, over time it could take her to new levels of understanding.

And how about the rest of us, the ones who watched Kristina's moment of triumph or who are reading about it right now—what are we to take from it?

At the end of her formal talk earlier that morning, the swami had told her assembled students to bring to mind a teaching, any teaching that moved us, and to contemplate that. Afterward, she told us that whatever we had settled on was our own teaching and that we ought to ruminate over it and discuss it with our friends, so that this personal teaching could truly enter us, could give us inspiration and guidance.

What happened with Kristina contains seminal instructions for me. I see myself in Kristina—see my shyness, my reluctance to take in the beauty life offers me, my tendency to ignore the jugglers and turn my back on the storytellers before me.

Something else the scene shows me is the swami's patience. I was delighted to watch her at play with Kristina, and to see how much energy and care she put into her extended gesture to reach one little girl. When one tack didn't work, the swami tried another, and on and on, until, finally, Kristina was happy, genuinely and undeniably happy.

My teacher has shown me an even greater patience than she did this three-year-old, for my instruction has been extended not over half an hour, as Kristina's was, but over the course of decades. You could say I'm a slow learner, but I prefer to look at it another way: the swami is an indefatigable teacher.

The most significant lesson for me is the last she offered the little girl: *look inside yourself.* By whatever means appeals to you, whatever means is available to you, with whatever energy you can muster, seek your satisfaction from within your own being. Or, you could say, *meditate.*

There are other lessons here as well, possibly as many as there are people to draw them. As the swami indicated earlier that morning, each is valid.

Acknowledgments

THIS STORY WOULD NEVER HAVE BEEN TOLD if I hadn't taken my old MacBook Pro to the reunion of the Whidbey Island Writers Association Lockdown Retreat in the spring of 2012. We were all, students and instructors alike, expected to share an excerpt from what we had written since the initial retreat. I'd been working on something, but it was at home on my new computer, so I read another piece, one I'd put aside because I was sure no one would be interested in it: an account of how, years before, I'd followed an Indian holy man.

The audience was enthralled. "What happens next?" people were saying, and, "You should write *this* book!" Since the topic is absolutely central to my life, I decided I would.

No book is the labor of just one person. *Learning to Eat Along the Way* received the encouragement, guidance, support, and felicitous criticism of a cadre of fellow scribes, both friends and professionals.

I am especially grateful to my editor, Elizabeth Kracht, who convinced me to expunge, explain, and expand much, and also to my copy editors, the artist and writer Jane Freeman and the retired journalist Deloris Tarzan Ament.

Others who read the entire manuscript at a go and offered support and astute suggestions are my dear friends and cohorts Lalli Dana Drobny, Laurel Murphy, Donna Hood, Pat Brunjes, Michele Coleman, Dorothy Read, Wendy Grove, Carol Overy,

Kris Collins, Yvonne Palka, Johnny Palka, and Judith Schafman.

Just as close to my heart, and of even greater benefit to my writing, are those friends who kindly, and sometimes repeatedly, allowed me to read various sections to them: Leah Green, Joyce Libby, Susanna Fest, and Deloris and Allan Ament.

There would have been no book, of course, without the swamis, to whom this work is dedicated. In the words of the poet-saint Kabir, "The guru is great beyond words, and great is the good fortune of the disciple." To these extraordinary teachers, my gratitude is lifelong.

Sources

The stories from the *Yoga Vasishtha* in chapter 13 ("The Story of Gadhi"), chapter 18 (the crow-and-the-coconut fragment from "The Story of King Janaka"), and the epilogue ("The Great Forest") are from the translation by Swami Venkatesananda, *Vasistha's Yoga* (Albany: State University of New York Press, 1993).

In chapter 17, statistics on the outcomes of anorexia nervosa are drawn from the South Carolina Department of Mental Health web page, "Eating Disorder Statistics," www.state.sc.us/dmh/anorexia/statistics.htm, last accessed November 2014.

The epilogue, "The Great Forest," appeared in an earlier version, "Re-entry," in the online magazine *Itineraries* and in the book *Journeys Outward, Journeys Inward*, both edited by Penelope Bourke (Chapel Hill, NC: Second Journey, 2013).

In the acknowledgments, the line from Kabir is from his poem "*sadgur soi daya kar dinha*, II. 81," translated by Rabindranath Tagore, *Songs of Kabir* (New York: The MacMillan Company, 1916), 76.

The photographs on pages 189 and 213 were taken by Grady Timmons.

About the Author

PHOTO CREDIT: BILL RUTH

MARGARET BENDET lives in the village of Langley on Whidbey Island in Washington State, where she handles freelance editing projects, teaches classes on memoir writing, attends a chanting and meditation group, picks blackberries (in season), and goes for walks with a small white dog named Chou Chou.

www.margaretbendet.com

SELECTED TITLES FROM SHE WRITES PRESS

She Writes Press is an independent publishing company founded to serve women writers everywhere. Visit us at www.shewritespress.com.

Where Have I Been All My Life? A Journey Toward Love and Wholeness by Cheryl Rice. $16.95, 978-1-63152-917-7. Rice's universally relatable story of how her mother's sudden death launched her on a journey into the deepest parts of grief—and, ultimately, toward love and wholeness.

Seeing Red: A Woman's Quest for Truth, Power, and the Sacred by Lone Morch. $16.95, 978-1-938314-12-4. One woman's journey over inner and outer mountains—a quest that takes her to the holy Mt. Kailas in Tibet, through a seven-year marriage, and into the arms of the fierce goddess Kali, where she discovers her powerful, feminine self.

Renewable: One Woman's Search for Simplicity, Faithfulness, and Hope by Eileen Flanagan. $16.95, 978-1-63152-968-9. At age forty-nine, Eileen Flanagan had an aching feeling that she wasn't living up to her youthful ideals or potential, so she started trying to change the world—and in doing so, she found the courage to change her life.

Fire Season: A Memoir by Hollye Dexter. $16.95, 978-1-63152-974-0. After she loses everything in a fire, Hollye Dexter's life spirals downward and she begins to unravel—but when she finds herself at the brink of losing her husband, she is forced to dig within herself for the strength to keep her family together.

Letting Go into Perfect Love: Discovering the Extraordinary After Abuse by Gwendolyn M. Plano. $16.95, 978-1-938314-74-2. After staying in an abusive marriage for twenty-five years, Gwen Plano finally broke free—and started down the long road toward healing.

Splitting the Difference: A Heart-Shaped Memoir by Tré Miller-Rodríguez. $19.95, 978-1-938314-20-9. When 34-year-old Tré Miller-Rodríguez's husband dies suddenly from a heart attack, her grief sends her on an unexpected journey that culminates in a reunion with the biological daughter she gave up at 18.